Paint
on paper

Paint
on paper

**Over 130 quick
and easy techniques
to decorate paper**

Angie Franke &
Monique Day-Wilde

D&C
David and Charles

A DAVID & CHARLES BOOK

David & Charles is an F+W Publications Inc.
company
4700 East Galbraith Road
Cincinnati, OH 45236

First published in the UK in 2008
First published in 2007 by Metz Press

ISBN-13: 978-0-7153-2953-5 paperback with flaps
ISBN-10: 0-7153-2953-7 paperback with flaps

Printed in China by WKT Company
for David & Charles
Brunel House   Newton Abbot   Devon

Visit our website at www.davidandcharles.co.uk

David & Charles books are available from all
good bookshops; alternatively you can contact
our Orderline on 0870 9908222 or write to us
at FREEPOST EX2 110, D&C Direct, Newton
Abbot, TQ12 4ZZ (no stamp required UK only);
US customers call 800-289-0963 and Canadian
customers call 800-840-5220.

Contents

Introduction

The roots of our paper experiences go back to our childhood when two special people sparked our interest and imagination by their exceptional skills with paper. As a small girl Monique was fascinated by the way in which her Aunt Monica took such care in wrapping her enormous pile of Christmas gifts – she knew a lot of people! The boxes, coloured paper, ribbons, bows and anything else that came to hand, made each a work of art, with small fingers to help tie bows and cut sticky tape. It's no wonder that some of this rubbed off – it's in the blood.

Angie's dad, Ted Cudmore, inspired her love for papier-mâché by making her a prize-winning astronaut's helmet from a balloon and torn newspaper for a fancy-dress party way back in 1968. His immense creativity with paper construction ranged from a nativity set enshrined in a painted and crumpled paper bag cave to a huge train set complete with stations and hilly country-side made from layers of cardboard and paper pulp. Even dainty silver stars from cigarette papers contributed to a wonderful legacy for his appreciative daughter and apprentice!

A few years ago we were asked to do some workshops to teach street children. The materials had to be affordable and preferably recyclable, so the obvious choice was paper! With the huge interest in paper crafts in general, the idea for this book was born.

This is a collection of ideas for paper decorating with the focus yet again on texture, line and colour. It encompasses a wide range of techniques gleaned from our pre-primary years through to more sophisticated inventions and ideas picked up on our combined creative journeys. We have generally used easily accessible copy paper and paints. The other bits and bobs such as tea leaves, sand, nail varnish, gold leaf and even crack filler, to mention a few, can be found round the house or sourced from art, craft and hardware stores – if not your veggie shop!

Paper is versatile, for the most part inexpensive and easy to decorate in a myriad ways. It is lightweight yet strong, can be torn, cut, folded, moulded, sculpted and even draped to create objects ranging from disposable nap-kins to weight-bearing bridges! There's so much out there just waiting to be decorated. We encourage you to explore using decorated paper for things other than printing, writing and gift wrapping. The patterns and ideas used to create the individual paper samples in this book are all simple, single tech-niques which become richer and more interesting, depending on how they are layered and applied. Create artworks such as mosaics and collages, make unique beads for jewellery, decorate boxes, funky masks, chandeliers, bowls, shoes and as many functional or quirky items as you can imagine.

Paper

The word *paper* is derived from the word *papyrus*, the name of a plant that was pounded and pulped and dried into flat sheets to produce one of the earliest known writing mediums used by the ancient Egyptians, Greeks and Romans. The birth of modern-day paper may be traced back to 105 AD, when a Chinese court official invented a paper-making process using rags, mulberry bark and hemp. The process was refined by adding sizing, coating and dyeing, as well as bamboo which was cooked in lye to separate the plant filaments. Chinese paper-making techniques spread to Korea and Japan where the secret remained for centuries. Paper is still made in these countries on a large scale today, mostly from mulberry bark.

The knowledge of paper-making eventually spread to the Arab countries where the techniques were improved by adding linen. Arabian paper was exported to Europe where paper-making only took off many centuries later. When Gutenberg invented the printing press and printed his first Bible around 1456 it was on parchment – specially prepared animal skin. One Bible required the skins of 300 sheep, and parchment could not be produced in high enough volumes to meet the demands of movable print.

European paper-makers now started pulping linen and canvas rags for paper. The increased demand for paper soon led to a shortage of raw materials necessitating more research into a substitute. The technique for producing pulp from trees was eventually developed in the mid 19th century. Mechanization made the production of paper faster and more economical but the process was only automated well into the 20th century when machine-made rolls of paper replaced hand-made sheets and paper was mass produced.

Right: These little bags were easy to make from decorated paper wrapped around a small box, and finished with ribbon, raffia or cord handles. The pink, yellow and blue paper was wet and coated with a thin layer of white PVA. Colours dragged across and down in the wet PVA with wide brushes, creating a dry-brush look. The colourful red and green bag was fabric painted with wide brushstrokes in every direction and textured with crumpled clingwrap laid over the wet paint. The paper for the blue bag was impressed with heavy linen to create a fabric texture. The lilac paper was washed in lavender acrylic paint, sprayed with water and left to dry – a simple technique great for background paper. Red and green fabric paint were mixed for the rusty-brown paper which was textured with a piece of scrunched up paper and sprinkled with gold dust.

Opposite page: Christine, a good friend and mosaic artist, made this paper mosaic from off-cuts of several other paper projects. She used a square punch and didn't have to grout – the grey backing board is a great substitute. The paper has a lot more texture than most tiles and is much easier to cut, so this is a great project for those who would like to try their hand at mosaics but don't have the strength for tile cutters.

Today paper is a high-tech product, available in every imaginable colour and finish. We may live in a so-called digital age, but we use just as much paper as before – from bathroom tissue and disposable napkins to packaging and billboards.

We are surrounded by paper in one form or another. It remains a convenient and durable option for storing information. Reading books will remain a great pleasure and artists will continue to express themselves on this versatile medium. Fortunately everybody is becoming aware of the depletion of our natural resources and the need to recycle paper wherever possible – this mindset needs to be encouraged in our own homes.

Acid-free paper

A lot has been said and written about acid-free paper and we don't want to get into a whole debate here. Briefly, acid-free paper has a neutral or pH of 7 or more. If prepared properly, paper made from any fibres can be acid free. Anything labelled archival should be acid and lignin free and the same goes for paper. If it has not had the acidity neutralized it will yellow and deteriorate with age. Acid migration can occur when neutral papers are exposed to pollutants or when two paper materials come in contact. For example, if a photo is adhered to paper with glue which has an acid content, it will yellow. Part of the printing process in photography involves acid. Although the paper would have been neutralized, there may be an acid residue. So, when

working with paper and related products, protect the precious things such as photos. But when it comes to transitory items such as cards and gift wrap, the acid content is hardly worth the mention!

DIY pH indicator

Try this easy DIY pH indicator paper project we've developed. You'll have a lot of fun testing different papers and substances for their acid or alkali content. The idea for this was initiated by trawling the Internet for information on plant dyes for use on paper. A children's science-project using pH neutral red cabbage juice sparked some creative energy and we are proud to include this as a unique and exciting way of home testing the pH level of any paper.

You need a red cabbage, a grater, water, filter paper or a fine sieve, a flat baking pan, blotting paper, a lemon, bicarbonate of soda and a few brushes.

1 Grate the cabbage and mix with a cup of water or blend in a liquidizer. Strain the juice through filter paper or a fine sieve into a flat baking pan.

2 Soak blotting paper in the juice for a minute, remove and dry flat on a protected surface. It should be pale purple-blue or lavender when dry.

3 Paint lines of neat and water-diluted lemon juice (acid) – these will turn the cabbage paper red and pink where they are painted, indicating degrees of acidity.

4 Dissolve bicarbonate of soda (alkali) into water, making a weak and a stronger solution and paint in alternating lines onto the cabbage paper. The strong solution will turn the paper yellow and the weaker solution will turn it green to blue.

5 Try painting lines of other household solutions such as bleach, tea, drain cleaner and so on to see what colours they produce.

Paint red cabbage juice onto various pieces of paper and see what colour the juice dries. This will indicate the acidity (pink to red) or alkalinity (blue/green to yellow) of the paper.

We tried it on newspaper and copy paper to test the two that are most commonly available and are pleased to announce that the copy paper we used throughout this book is neutral or acid-free.

Follow the steps on this page and make your own testing paper to try out paints and additions you want to use if you are concerned about acidity.

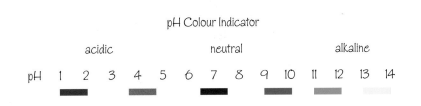

pH Colour Indicator

acidic   neutral   alkaline

pH 1 2 3 4 5 6 7 8 9 10 11 12 13 14

Types of paper

Papyrus is the mother of paper and is still around today. Buy it at good craft shops and use it for that special calligraphy project.

Handmade paper can be produced from just about any fibre or fibrous plant as paper is simply matted fibres. Paper pulp is made from the raw material and water, and scooped up onto a frame. The water is allowed to drain and the pulp is then couched and pressed (turned out from the frame). The pressed sheets are laid out on interfacing and wads of newspaper to dry. There is a lot of information available about handmade paper which can be an exciting and very affordable home craft.

Rice paper usually refers to paper made from the rice plant, though the term is also loosely associated with paper made with other plant materials like hemp, bamboo or mulberry.

Mulberry paper is also known as Kozo paper. It is not very absorbent, but may take some light drawing with very little erasure. It is generally used for linoleum and woodblock printing, and is a popular choice for luminaire decoupage.

Water-colour paper has a high cotton-fibre content and comes in many different sizes, weights and packages, such as pads and blocks. A water-colour block is a stack of water-colour paper gummed together at the edges. This makes it possible to paint without pre wetting and stretching the paper, as is usually required for thinner papers. Completed paintings should air dry on the block, without the help of the sun or a blow drier. Small pieces of water-colour paper, decorated with miniature paintings, make good subjects for special cards which can be preserved in frames. There are three categories of finishes which vary from brand to brand:

- Hot press has a smooth surface and is excellent for soft drawing materials, pen and ink, brush line-work, wash, and airbrush.
- Cold press, or semi-rough, is the most popular finish and is excellent for traditional water-colour techniques, charcoal, pastel, and paint sticks. A sense of depth can be created with the texture in water-colour paper, and many textural effects can be developed with a minimum of effort.
- Rough finish has pronounced peaks and valleys and is more difficult to use – even wet washes tend to be speckled with some spots of white showing through. Rough finish paper can be used effectively with acrylics, paint sticks, and some pastels. This paper is usually less expensive.

Cartridge paper is a high quality, heavy paper used for illustration and drawing and is freely available in art and craft shops. It was originally used for making weaponry cartridges, hence the name. We would rather use it for funky shoes!

Drawing paper is any paper on which a mark may be made with drawing materials such as charcoal or graphite. It must be durable enough to take repeated erasure without damaging the surface, and it should take ink without excessive bleeding. It varies widely in quality from newsprint to fine, handmade Fabriano paper and can be categorized into several groups:

- Bristol paper comes in two finishes, plate and vellum, in several thicknesses and is the most durable all-purpose drawing paper available. Plate finish is very smooth and works well for pen and ink, and airbrushing, allowing for flat and even washes. The finish is too slick for coloured pencil, charcoal, pastel, and very soft pencil. Vellum is an all-purpose finish.
- Charcoal or pastel paper comes in a variety of colours and finishes and serves the same purpose as water-colour paper. The paper has little sizing and is not very durable, taking only light erasing before being damaged. Ingres and Canson are examples of this paper. We've used these coloured papers as backgrounds for some of our examples and they make excellent card stock.

Opposite page: Our fan was made in sections with an array of different examples, chosen for colour and texture, from the multitude of paper possibilities. From left to right we used sisal, stained handmade paper, brown paper, Japanese lace paper threaded with coir fibres, leaf-embedded, tracing, elephant-dung, copy and mulberry paper, vellum, tissue, handmade paper, embossed and water-colour paper, crumpled pearl-coated paper, silk paper, Canson, papyrus and gold-coated paper.

- Bond paper comes in different finishes and has good strength and stiffness. The name was originally given to paper which was used for printing bonds and stock certificates. It is mostly used for good stationery. Decorate sheets of bond paper and use it as special writing paper.

Interleaving is pH neutral and non-abrasive separation sheets used to isolate artworks on paper from their containers, or protect surfaces in handling (for example the tissue between layers of gold leaf).

Calligraphy paper will not easily bleed, feather, scratch, or wrinkle when used with pen and ink.

Blotting paper is any absorbent un-sized paper which can be used to soak up excess ink or oil. (We looked this up in the Wikipedia and found this interesting snippet: "When used to remove ink from writings, the writing may appear in reverse on the surface of the blotting paper, a phenomenon which has been used as a plot device in a number of detective stories.")

Coated papers are available in many different finishes, including metallic and adhesive-backed, but few are archival. They may be used for bookbinding, printing, presentations, mock-ups, architectural models, and so on.

Transfer papers such as graphite or carbon paper are used to transfer a drawing or writing to another surface. Some carbon papers are coated with dry, impressionable ink which does not erase well once applied, but transfers onto non-porous

surfaces, such as metal, better than graphite. Printing transfer papers can be used with digital printers.

Photo papers are specially coated to ensure that the ink 'sits' on the paper rather than being absorbed by it. These papers are for use in inkjet printers to make digital prints. They can be glossy or matt.

Cover paper is used in the printing industry for covers of magazines, booklets and catalogues. The better grades have good light fastness, are quite durable, and make fine drawing and calligraphy paper.

Transparent or translucent paper is usually not archival owing to the processes and chemicals used in making them translucent or transparent.

- Tracing paper is impregnated with a resin or an oil to make it transparent. The lesser quality tracing paper will not take erasure well, leaving a faint impression. This works beautifully inside decorated paper lanterns as it diffuses light softly. Use it as a more economical substitute for vellum.
- Greaseproof paper (not to be confused with wax wrap) is a strong, transparent kitchen paper which takes dye, crayons and pastels fairly well and can be used as an inexpensive substitute for tracing paper. Try dip dyeing with this paper as it is much stronger than tissue paper.
- Baking parchment is silicone coated and therefore non-stick. It makes a wonderful transfer paper for oil pastels.
- Wax wrap can be drawn on with any oil or wax-based crayon. It

can be painted or stencilled on the non-wax side for unusually attractive wrapping paper, or used in collages. Crumpling and ironing the paper results in a delicate transparent crackle which is particularly effective over darker coloured papers.

- Vellum refers to a good quality tracing paper which is most popular with scrapbookers and card makers. Ink may be scraped off the paper with a blade without seriously disturbing the surface. This paper takes all drawing media well. It is especially good for pen and ink but is easily affected by moisture and skin oils. It tears and cracks easily and does not age well. We have used it for a classy gift bag and an exotic curtain.
- Graphics paper makes exceptional drawing paper and has been especially improved for work with permanent markers. It may be opaque or particularly translucent – more so than tracing paper – It and has a bright, white appearance.

Opposite page: The cone gift-wrappings were folded from sheets of paper decorated with fabric paint – flogging in lilac, malachite in green, scrunching off in purple and lapis lazuli in blue. Stamps created with bits of junk from the garage were used for the stamped paper. The box sides were covered with dragged greens and the lid with more green malachite paper, all varnished for strength. Line paper cones with greaseproof and tissue papers for edible gifts.

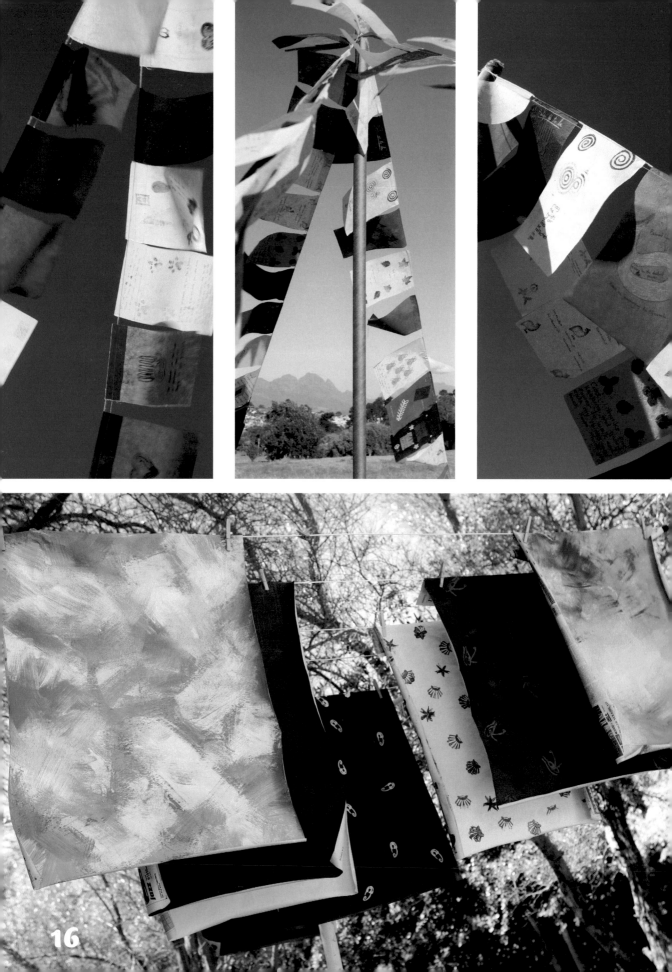

Tissue paper is very thin but good quality tissue paper is quite strong. It is available in a range of wonderful colours and is useful for a variety of projects besides wrapping. We used it for a dip-dye technique (see pages 74-75).

Interfacing is a very thin non-woven material, usually used for strengthening fabric. It is made from polyester and may also be used in various applications traditionally reserved for paper, such as sewing patterns. Interfacing can be used to strengthen flimsy artworks, where many layers or small bits of paper have been put together. It comes in different strengths and finishes, some with iron-on fusible adhesive. It takes paint very well and we have made our flags with the spun bond variety.

Stencil paper is either waxed or oiled to prevent it from buckling when used repeatedly with water-based paints. Drafting polyester has at least one side chemically treated so that one can draw on it and has become popular for making more durable stencils. It is not affected by moisture; it will lie flat even after being rolled up for a long time and it will not tear.

Backing or release paper is commonly used as a base for stickers and contact or adhesive paper. This slippery paper is coated on one or both sides, for example polyester-coated freezer paper, and is very useful for making stencils which can be cut and ironed in position (slippery side down) onto other paper temporarily.

Brown paper is strong and economical and is traditionally used for different types of parcels and bags. It is available in different weights, from strong, cardboard-like corrugated paper to thinner sheets suitable for wrapping fragile items. We give it a thumbs up for recycling and decorating. We've used this as a base for masks and bowls but with black stamped motifs it can't be beaten for that ethnic look wrapping paper.

Printing or copy paper is used mostly in the office environment. It is mass produced and relatively inexpensive. With the industry being ever more aware of pH levels, most of this paper is nearly acid free. Large sheets or rolls are available from copy shops and can be used to make your own wrapping paper. We have used this extensively.

Paper towelling and serviettes are soft, layered paper. They absorb dye well and can be strengthened with varnish and used for decoupage and other art needs such as papier-mâché and blotting. Toilet paper and tissues are slightly thinner and can be used successfully for papier-mâché and paper making as they dissolve so easily. We always have some handy to mop up any spills in our studios.

Newspaper is the cheapest and most widely available type of paper but is non-archival which means it doesn't last. It has a high lignin content which causes the paper to become brittle and yellow with age or when exposed to sunlight. It is used in the printing of newspapers, flyers and other printed material which is not intended to last. While newspaper is not recommended for recycling by making handmade paper (because of the acid and the black dye in the printing inks), it can be recycled for other creative purposes such as papier-mâché.

Our favourite simple suggestion is that you paint sheets of newspaper with leftover PVA wall paints when you've finished decorating somewhere in your home. This makes completely unique and inexpensive gift wrap – besides the simple therapy of sloshing paint on paper! The PVA obliterates the printing ink and adds strength to the flimsy newspaper, resulting in something interesting and useful (see opposite page bottom).

Opposite page top: We both live in windy unpolluted areas so getting friendship flags fluttering and flapping was a breeze and brought much joy to all who participated. Here more than 200 flags are offering their blessings to the elements. Many friends cottoned on to this take on traditional prayer flags. We all fabric painted spun-bond paper in five traditional colours for air (white), earth (yellow), sky (blue), water (green) and fire (red). We stamped our flags with black and white images and wrote blessings and requests with white pencil crayons and milky pens and permanent black markers. This is a great idea for collaborative art projects for schools and groups – or even for friends to mark special occasions such as the birth of a baby, weddings, special birthdays and anniversaries.

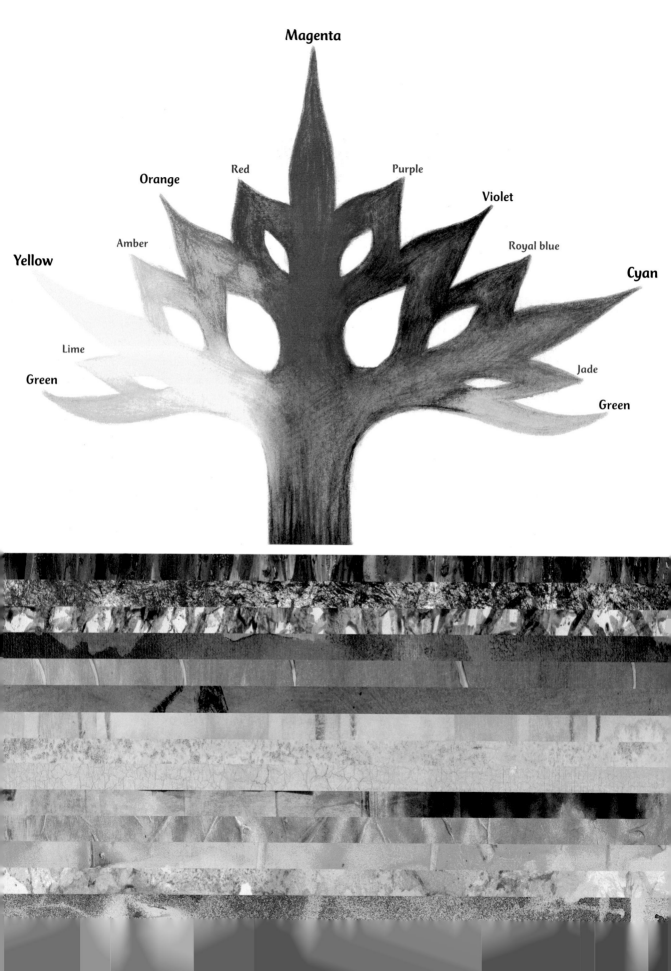

Colour

Mixing your own paints is a great way to learn about colour relationships. There isn't a colour range in the world that always has the particular colour you're looking for, so play around with mixing the colours you want. You may also want to paint your own colour wheel as it will be your most useful colour-reference tool.

Hues

Yellow, magenta (red) and cyan (blue) are the primary colours or hues used for digital and other printing. The colour family-tree on the opposite page illustrates the basic colour relationships.

Secondary colours or hues are green, orange and violet, while the tertiary colours or hues are lime, amber, red, purple, royal blue and jade. Colours are further developed as follows:

Tints

A tint is a hue with white added to make a pastel. Many degrees of tints can be obtained, depending on how much white is added to a hue.

Shades

A shade is a hue with grey or black added in small quantities to tone it. The depth of shade will depend on the amount of black added.

Earth tones and neutrals

To bring in earth tones (variations of brown) or neutral colours, we mix hues of complementary colours. Complementary in this sense literally means the colours which are found opposite each other on the colour wheel, namely yellow and violet, magenta and green, cyan and orange, lime and purple, jade and red, royal blue and amber.

When used together, these colours work well as a contrast, and are a good choice as they complement and accent each other. Small quantities of a colour may be mixed with a complementary hue to tone the colour from bright and sharp to muted and earthy: magenta with a small amount of green makes maroon. These colours may also be turned into pastels with the addition of white, or toned to shades by adding black or grey.

Brown

If you mix the primary colours in differing ratios you will get browns ranging from khaki through various chocolate browns. You may also find the mix becoming grey, even though you didn't use black. Creams and skin tones are mixed by adding various browns to white.

Colour combinations

Harmonious or analogous colours lie next to each other on the colour wheel. When deciding on a colour combination, it is always safe to work with triangular patterns, for example two harmonies spiked with one accent (complementary). Lighter and darker tones of the same colour live in harmony with each other and are comfortable on the eye. More exciting, though, are combinations that make use of a pair of complementary colours such as cyan (blue) and orange, or green and magenta (red).

The warm colours are the magenta/red/orange/yellow half of the colour wheel, while the blue/green/purple/violet half is the cooler colours. Cool colours are calming and recede in combinations, while warmer colours are inviting and exciting.

Mixing colour

The paint techniques which constitute the rest of the book have been done in groups of colours through the entire spectrum of the colour wheel. The colours were made up as listed below. Please note that these ratios may need adjusting according to the strength of pigments or paints used. Remember our golden rule: experiment and have fun. After all, you can never have too many browns!

We used the primaries, as well as the following mixed colours:

purple:	2 magenta + 1 violet
violet:	1 cyan + 1 magenta
royal:	1 violet + 2 blue
blue:	5 cyan + 1 magenta
jade:	1 cyan + 1 green
green:	1 cyan + 1 yellow
lime:	1 yellow + 1 green
sepia:	1 cyan + 3 orange + 5 white
brown:	3 yellow + 2 magenta + 1 cyan
gold:	6 yellow + 1 purple
amber:	3 yellow + 1 orange
orange:	4 yellow + 1 red
red:	2 magenta + 1 yellow

Patterns

While we have described this section as "patterns", the accent is really on the mediums and tools used. Our examples are illustrations of some of the paints and tools not used much in the rest of this book. Pattern is the repetition of a design or motif and we have chosen these specific mediums and tools as set out on the following pages to excite your interest.

Top right: These lacquer crackers were a cinch to make. We found the ready-made glossy cut-outs at a party shop and all we had to do was dilute a little glass paint, glitter and nail varnish with acetone, swirl the mix together and throw it on! It dried in minutes … A great way to package small precious gifts or wow your dinner guests.

Right: I have always wanted a pair of paper shoes – just for fun – so I jumped at the chance of making some for this book. I decorated the paper by stamping a square patterned stamp onto it with fabric paint extender. Once dry, I painted all over it with a maroon wash adding pure red in places. The paper turned out quite mottled, which was just what I wanted. The woven shoe fronts were finished off with gold-dragged paper along the edges, with a stamped, embossed detail on the top. The weave pattern is similar to that used for the baskets on page 133.

Bottom right: Heather Laithwaite of Dare to bead fame made this glass marker, held onto the glass stem with magnetic beads at the back. She used beads made from fabric-painted paper – off-cuts from another project put to good use. These beads were embossed with sparkly embossing powder which worked well with the purple in the paper. Paper beads combine really well with glass and other beads.

Opposite page: Using plaster of Paris moulds of our faces we made papier-mâché masks and had great fun decorating them. Monique chose a butterfly as inspiration, decorating her mask with small off-cuts of fabric-painted paper glued in position with wallpaper glue. Linear detail in a gold glitter pen and fine pearl glitter glue smeared over the pink area added to the shine, with the final dramatic effect coming from wire embellishments at the top of the head. Angie's beloved ginger cat inspired her brown-paper covered mask adorned with a vast range of scraps applied over a wash of transparent orange fabric paint: burn-marked paper on the ears and cheeks, cracked-paint paper on the forehead, cheekbones and chin; dip-dyed green paper eyeshadows; random red and orange dragged bits on the nose and jowls; silver and blue mosaic-stamped paper on the sides. Defining lines and dots were added in magenta, blue, green, gold and silver glitter glue.

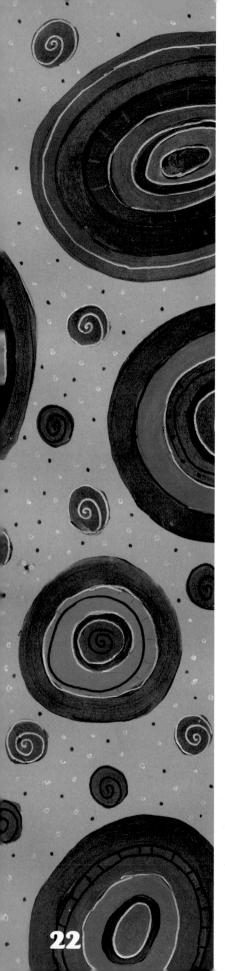

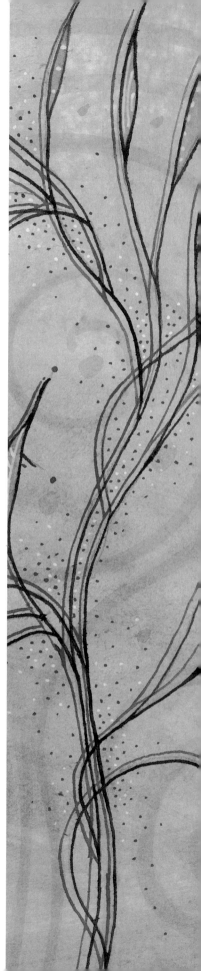

Mediums

Most paints and mediums can be applied directly onto paper. They usually consist of a colour (pigment), mixed with a glue (base). Generally, paints are either water based or oil based. We have included general descriptions of and application instructions for various paints but it is always important to follow the specific manufacturer's instructions for their particular products.

Acrylic

These paints are economical and are available in a wide range of colours, quantities and qualities, including craft and artist acrylics as well as ordinary PVA. While they may be diluted with water when liquid, they are permanent and water resistant when dry. They are mostly opaque unless mixed with glazes to render them transparent.

For our sample (see opposite page left) we've painted a "zooty" pattern of flying saucers in the twilight zone with detail added in milky pens. We used small flat brushes to paint concentric circles and ovals in harmonizing tones of purple and maroon craft paint. Fine silver milky pen lines and dots highlight the design and add interest to the background. This paper will add interest to any card or scrapbooking page.

Fabric paint

Fabric paint is also acrylic based but deserves special mention as it has a softer emulsion base which leaves a sheen on the paper surface and dries to a flexible finish.

We have used fabric paint throughout this book for various papers and projects – among others almost all the papers in the brown faux finishes section. It was also used to create the vibrant-coloured wrapping papers on page 121.

Pigment dyes

Also called sun or silk paints, these are made from pigment bound with liquid fixer. They can be sprayed, wet painted and used for paint-on-dye techniques. They have strong colours and may be diluted to achieve paler results.

On heavier paper, the dye will flow easier if you wet the surface first. These dyes can be used with fine stencil work if sprayed with an atomizer, airbrush or toothbrush to fill in stencils. Find our examples on pages 116-119. Water techniques look great with light shining through them and make beautiful lanterns and lampshades.

Water colour

These may be bought in flat pans or in artists' tubes and are available in many qualities. These paints are also very economical and portable. They are most suitable for finer projects which require soft colouring, for example landscape miniatures suitable for cards or simple calendars.

Inks

Inks are mostly water based and are available in permanent and washable finish. Their colours are generally vibrant but can be softened by adding water. Inks are suitable for washes and fine work with pens and brushes and may be sprayed, for example through airbrushes and spray bottles. As inks are most often used as an illustrative medium used an ornamental image in our example (see opposite page right). This paper was washed with diluted ink and a large water-colour brush for a soft background which was detailed with spirals using a smaller brush when the wash was dry. The ornamental grass design was drawn with a fine pen in purple and magenta ink. Dots and details, in the same colours and opaque white were added for interest. Designs like these work well for general greeting cards.

Glazes

Glazes are basically paints thinned with their relevant solvents, with the addition of neutral glaze to delay drying time. This enables them to be worked into textural effects. Glazes are transparent, adding depth to the base coat, and drying to a soft sheen. The papers for the chess and backgammon games (see pages 86-87) were created using acrylic scumble glaze and PVA paints. For a basic glaze mix 1 part PVA, 1 part sumble glaze and 1 part water.

Oil paints

Artists' oil-paints are flexible and long lasting but are not normally used on paper. They dry

24

to a smooth, shiny finish. Artists' oil-paints are not cheap, but can be thinned with turpentine to achieve interesting washes and more transparent effects quite economically. They come in a wide colour range and are available in small quantities. Oil paints can also be used as an alternative to lino printing ink. A new range of water soluble oils is becoming popular and makes this medium more user friendly. Monique's face mask on the author photo was painted with a variety of oil colours to simulate skin tones.

Spray paint

Spray paint is available in many finishes including enamel, antique, metallic and a wide range of colours including neon and fluorescent. It has the advantage of easy application. No mess, no fuss! We used spraypaint on the paper on page 116. It was also used to create the encrusted gold finish on the crown in the mad hatter's tea party (see page 37). Clear lacquer spray has been used as an easy, quick drying varnish in many of our finished projects.

Food colouring

These are economical and edible inks and can be used in as many ways as normal ink. The colour range is limited but if you know how, they can be mixed to any hue your heart desires. These are an economical alternative for calligraphers. Our example shown here was done with calligraphy pens (see opposite page middle and description under calligraphy pens on page 27).

Others

There are also odd paints and mediums not normally used on paper that deserve mention, and though we have not used them all in this book, we encourage you to give them a try.

Rust paint is designed to look corroded and rusted (see pages 124-125).

Copper paint is virtually the same type of paint as rust paint but has an aged patina and verdigris (green/blue) colour. We suggest painting it onto a papier-mâché bowl to simulate an authentic copper finish.

Metallics are shiny paints which can also be home made by adding metallic powder to glaze. We have used them extensively in the metallic section and also in a few of our paper items such as the beads, boxes and shoes.

Pearl paints are similar to metallics, but use powdered mica (pearl powders), to produce a lovely soft lustre. Pigments may be added, but as the mica is white based, they will result in pastel tones. We used pale gold pearl to soften the dark brown on the Rooibos tea-bags on our quick art project on pages 104-105.

Sparkle/glitter paints have coloured glitter or sparkle dust mixed into them. We've used sparkle dust onto wet paint on the wine box and some wrapping paper.

Neon paints look bright and synthetic. They are very appealing and funky for pop art and children's projects. Rather expensive, they are available in bottles and spray cans. This ball-point pen doodle (opposite page right) has a neon painted background and is detailed with pearl paint.

Glow in the dark (fluorescent paint) is water based and glows gently after being charged by shining bright light on the painted area. This would be fun for a Halloween project or a starry paper mobile.

Glass paints are available as solvent or water-based paints. They usually dry clear with a shiny finish if applied thickly on shiny paper, though this has a tendency to crack if flexed. Stiffer paper is recommended. Frosted, opaque and textured variations are also available. Thin with the relevant solvent for better absorption on paper. We used blue, yellow and magenta solvent-based glass paint for our laminated vellum curtain on page 5.

Nail varnishes from the cosmetic bargain bins in your local supermarket could supply a constant flow of shiny supplements to your paint palette. These are most effective when diluted with acetone or nail varnish remover, but lacquer thinners will also do the job. The colour range is as vast and sparkly as are most current fashion accessories.

For our sample page opposite left we used the small nail-varnish brushes to paint silver, magenta and purple stripes of sparkly and glitter nail varnish onto glossy paper. For extra depth we added maroon glass paint with a fine water-colour brush to this example. We have also used nail varnishes in the amber marbling section on page 112 and to decorate our party crackers (see page 20).

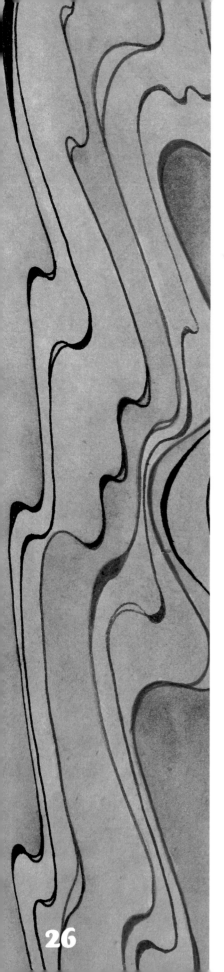

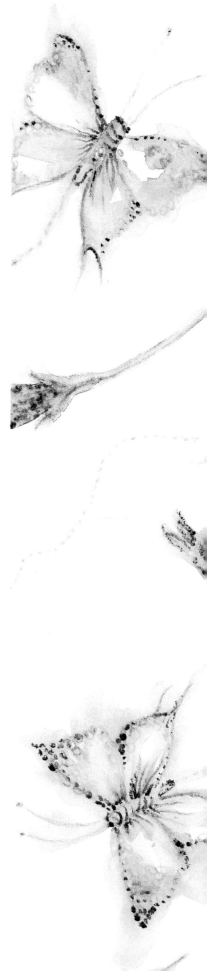

Tools

We have used many tools – from keys to rollers – to decorate our papers. The following are the most conventional and widely used:

Pens and pencils

Pens and pencils in one form or another have been around as long as paper, from the simple wedge-shaped stylus and the feather quill to sophisticated fountain and ball-point pens.

Calligraphy pens are specialized dipping pens – grown-up feather quills – available in varying nibs sizes to create beautiful writing. They can also be used to create all sorts of patterns like ours on page 24: a simple motif repeated across the page with food colouring as ink. Graph paper was used under the paper to keep the pattern straight. The basic pattern is a combination of crosses joined by s-shapes in a grid formation. The broad calligraphy pen nib was used at the same angle throughout the design. The cross shape comprises five short-angled strokes joined together – one in the middle and one on each axis. A few rows of this design would make an interesting border for a plain white gift bag.

Fibre-tip pens, also known as kokis, have an absorbent fibre core and compressed fibre tip. They are available in washable, permanent, neon (highlighters), vanishing, metallic and even scented inks in a huge range of colours. In our example we used the conventional type adding shading with coloured inks.

Fibre-tip pens are very versatile and come in varying qualities:

- Economical bold, bright packs for children's school and art work;
- Expensive calligraphy and other specialized pens with different tips, such as brush, wedge or bullet pointed;
- More gimmicky varieties such as stamp-tipped and spray or blow pens.

Make your own fibre-tip pens using cake decorating koki blanks for food colouring, or by recycling old ones. Remove the soft fibre core and tip from pens that are able to open and soak them in ink or food colouring for several hours or until saturated. Reassemble the pen and shake well. Leave standing with point down for at least an hour before using so that gravity encourages the ink-flow.

Ballpoint pens are two a penny and mostly available in blue, black and red. We haven't used them much here as we use them all the time on paper for more boring work – don't rule them out, though. The fine lines are great for doodling and cross-hatching and, of course, writing!

Gel pens are a variation of ball points using gel inks which come in many colours and finishes, from transparent to opaque and metallic, permanent and washable. Milky pens are generally opaque and permanent. Because they have a white, milky base, the colours are softer or pastel. These look great on dark paper – especially the metallics. We used them to highlight the acrylic paint design on page 22.

Graphite pencils are rated from hard (H) which don't smudge and make light marks on paper, to soft (B) which make darker markings. The higher the number, the more easily the pencil smudges. The example of the cartoon cats shown here (opposite page middle) uses the whole range of hard to soft pencils with the background washed in aquarelles. The fishy dream bubbles were added with traditional indelible marking pencil which turns purple when washed with water. This cute design would be just perfect for wrapping paper to woo any cat lover.

Aquarelle pencils are water-soluble and are good water-colour substitutes. They can be used in a number of ways: on wet paper, dipped in water or with moisture applied after application. The lavender and butterfly sample was made with dots, dashes and other purple, lilac and pink aquarelle pencil strokes on aquarelle paper. A fine water-colour brush was used to paint water softly over the edges to create a fluttery impression. Further detail was added in the same aquarelle colours while the paper was wet. This resulted in much darker, more definite lines. A feminine design like this could be colour copied onto A3 sheets and used as pretty drawer liner or wrapping paper.

Coloured pencils are available in a wide range of qualities. It's best to buy the more expensive artist's type as they sharpen without breaking and their colours are more intense. While you're at, it invest in a decent sharpener too!

For the sample on the opposite page left we have used pink, purple and violet pencils on graph paper to build up this repeating design of stars. Colouring it in a different way would produce a completely different look.

Charcoal drawing sticks or pencils are made from charcoal powder combined with a gum binder. The amount of binder determines the hardness. The drawing sticks produce soft black lines which smudge very easily. The powder can be used alone to cover large areas with grey tones. These can be drawn over or erased for effect. Seal the finished work with hairspray or fixative.

A charcoal pencil was used to create the shaded effect on this bold design (see opposite page middle), drawn on lilac mulberry paper. Extra colour was added with a pencil crayon to enhance the shapes. A simple graphic designs such as this would make great greeting cards, if sealed with a suitable fixative.

Crayons

Various types of crayons are most useful paper decorating tools.

White and coloured chalks leave soft, powdery marks when used for drawing on paper. These can be blended using a torchon (a blending tool of tightly rolled paper). Chalks work best on paper which has a bit of 'tooth' to grip it.

Finished work needs to be sealed with a suitable fixative such as clear lacquer spray.

Our triangle sample (opposite page right) was drawn with purple, pink and lilac chalks. It was blended using fingers and softened with a hake brush. A quickly chalked design is really suitable for disposable paper such as gift wrap as the chalk wears off easily.

Pastel crayons can be chalk or oil-based and are available in a wide range of colours, shapes and intensities. They can be bought in sets or individually and work best on darker paper with texture. Oil pastels can be blended with a torchon and washed over with turpentine for a subtle effect. Pastel examples are included in the oil and wax range of papers (see pages 58-63).

Beeswax crayons are mostly used for special effects such as encaustic work, but the good old junior-school variety works well for many projects. Retractable crayon sticks (those encased in plastic holders) are less waxy and produce smoother effects on paper.

Brushstrokes

Brushes come in many shapes and sizes. The most obvious use is to paint solid colour flat on paper or draw lines, but why not be adventurous and experiment! Use wall-painting brushes to produce interesting effects. Try softening all sorts of paint effects using a hake brush. We've used a variety of brushes in different ways throughout the book. In this section we show you some samples of basic brushstroke effects which can be achieved with the most ordinary brushes:

Top right: The paper for this collection was created in magenta, blue and a deep, rich purple. The wine box paper was painted with a very large brush in haphazard strokes, and sprinkled with silver powder while the paint was still wet to create a stardust feel. The tray was decoupaged with royal blue painted paper leaf printed in layers using silver, dark blue, opaque lilac, purple and magenta screen-printing inks. A sticky-backed wine bottle label was painted in washes of permanent drawing inks over a spattering of latex resist to simulate a starry sky. Decoupaged coasters boast paper finished in various faux techniques. Paper with the same finishes was used for weaving the placemats: wood-graining, flogging, scrunching-off, bagging-on, lapis lazuli and faux marble.

Right: These hat boxes were a real bargain, but in serious need of redecoration. I used a stencil for the smaller one's paper which I painted with white. When this was dry, I scraped the paper all over with a credit card, using blue and then watered down blue-grey acrylic paint. The same colours were used to paint in the design on the paper for the larger box, adding a deep blue-grey in the background. I painted red into this while it was still wet, to add to the texture. The slightly three-dimensional effect was enhanced by adding white highlights to the upper areas of the design, while shadows were created by adding very dark grey underneath.

Bottom right: A rectangular box wrapped in paper with a more masculine design. The paper was painted roughly with purple and green acrylic paint which was then printed over in silver using a handmade stamp. The stamp was made by impressing a large nut into a mouldable foam block heated with a heat gun. We added to the theme by using wire, nuts and washers rather than ribbons and bows to embellish the gift.

Opposite page: A tree filled with paper leaves would add pizzazz to any party scene. Various patterns were used in the lilac, pink and blue colour-range, from scraping and printed mosaic to oil and shaving-cream marbling. We first made templates of various leaf sizes and traced them onto a few sheets of patterned paper. These were used as top sheets which made cutting out much easier and quicker.

Dry-brushing

Dry-brushed paper makes an interesting textured looking paper suitable for end papers in handmade books. We used this inside our scrapbooking album cover. It creates a soft effect rather than solid colour. A stiff-bristled brush of any size can be used for dry brushing.

1 Dip your brush in paint and brush over a styrofoam punnet to get rid of the excess paint, allowing the bristles to absorb the paint.

2 Drag the 'dry' brush over clean paper in any direction until the desired texture is achieved.

Dragging

Dragging creates a fine linear effect, similar to wood grain, without the knots. We used it to decorate the sides of boxes which have more decorative lids, as it complements a busy design. It is, however, very effective on its own. Subtle colour variations can be achieved by blending different colours while dragging. This technique works best on damp, primed paper.

1 Either spray a small amount of water onto the page or cover with extender or glaze.

2 Drag a paint-loaded brush in one direction leaving fine parallel lines showing.

3 Repeat until the page has been covered and leave to dry.

Stippling

Our example was stippled in one colour, but blending layers of different colours works well for this technique, as in the fine granite effect on the chess board on page 87. Rich, deep textures may be built up this way. A large or fat wall-paint brush is best for this technique. Small, stiff brushes may also be used, but will take a long time to cover a sizeable area.

1 Place blobs of paint on a sheet of paper and work the paint into the bristles of a large brush.

2 Tap the ends of the bristles lightly onto the paper to build up a speckled texture.

34

Daubing

Don't overdo this technique or you'll lose the effect. Work with a light wrist action and keep it simple. You can always add colour if you find the effect too sparse. Daubing creates quick mottled wrapping paper. Regular daub marks result in any number of interesting patterns.

1 Load a flat brush with paint in your colour of choice.

2 Dab the entire brush onto the paper creating a mottled, splodgey effect as the bristles splay out on contact.

3 Repeat the process with more colours if you wish.

Swirling

Depending on the colours used, the swirls could depict floral designs such as roses, or watery designs such as curling waves. Again, blending colours in this fashion, gives unique results. As the wrist action required leaves bolder marks, we suggest using this technique for larger items. This technique works very well with fabric paint. Use more than one colour for depth.

1 Twirl a paint-loaded brush all over the paper.

2 Twist and spiral the paint quite thickly to show off the brush strokes.

Brush stamping

This technique works best with round stencil brushes of different sizes and can be used through stencils, or simply to cover a small sheet of paper with a more definite stippled pattern. This works well for any small area requiring interesting texture, for example paper to be made into beads.

1 Stamp paint-loaded bristles directly down onto paper.

2 Repeat randomly in varying colours and sizes for more interest.

Stamping

This is the simplest way to repeat designs on paper and it offers much scope for paper decorating. We used a variety of bought and home-made stamps and printing blocks to create our sample papers with different techniques. Here are some general tips for successful printing:

- Make sure you have an even surface for printing – slightly padded is best, for example on a pile of magazines or newspapers for a bit of give.
- Use even pressure on your print block or stamp. If you use found objects, cover them with a wooden block or rigid piece of plastic to apply pressure evenly.
- Determine beforehand whether transparent or opaque ink will work best for the surface you are printing. Light, transparent colours will not show up on dark paper but may be used as a base for embossing or flocking powders to adhere to.
- Besides bought stamp pads you can create your own inking surfaces by using absorbent materials such as felt, sponge or polystyrene punnets. Sheer surfaces such as glass, acrylic or plastic sheeting work well when printing with feathers or other absorbent stamps.

Opposite page and right: There's no time like tea time and that's any time! So why not host a mad hatter's tea party with decorated paper? The table runners were both painted in fabric paint – one striped, using different widths of paintbrushes, the other scrunched off and printed with a square sponge when dry to create a harlequin pattern. The thick paper serviettes were printed with a conventional stamp pad and a small round stamp. The mad hatter's headgear was made from marbled paper on the crown and brim, darkened in places with paint and a brush. The sides were dragged, and chalk striped paper was used as a band, all finished off with glitter glue and twisted paper. Dragged and dry-brushed paper in various colours were used for the red bonnet while the white bowler, constructed from spackle-sealed-papier mâché over a styrofoam pizza plate, was decorated with a purple ribbon fabric-painted in rough strokes and stamped over with red puff paint leaves.

The cat-in-the-hat hat is a paper potato sack … I painted broad red and white PVA stripes around it and the cardboard rim and added a cartoon effect with thin black lines in craft paint. Puff paint hearts decorate the red crêpe-paper lining of the Queen of Hearts crown. Fake ermine formed by stamping brown markings on white embossed paper towelling forms the padded base for the card-constructed headpiece, where further embellishments in gold spray-paint, gold sparkle dust, glitter, red glass-paint and nail varnish all add their shine.

38

Natural objects

Feathers, leaves and vegetables make good stamps. These pointers will help you achieve success with stamping or printing feathers and leaves or any other flat object that can't easily be held while inking:

1. Roll or sponge ink onto a flat surface instead of a stamp pad. Place the printing object onto the inked surface – vein side down for detailed stamping. Cover the object with a sheet of kitchen paper and rub over it gently.

2. Remove the kitchen paper, lift the object carefully off the inked surface and place it inked side down onto your paper. Cover with clean kitchen paper and rub or roll over it again to ensure an even print. Lift object off the surface carefully and dry or emboss the image.

We printed with opaque white fabric paint on dark paper.

Hand-carved stamps

Stamps can be carved with a blade or sharp knife from objects such as potatoes or erasers. Remember when carving to reverse your image so that it will print the right way – this is especially important with lettering. We used a potato and the discarded off-cuts for the crazy baobab style stamp patterns:

1. Cut potato cleanly in half with a sharp knife with a smooth blade (not serrated) and place onto absorbent paper for a few minutes to dry. It is important that the cut surface is evenly flat or it will not print properly. Draw a simple image onto the dry potato surface and cut away the parts around the design so that the image stands out at least 5 mm.

2. Ink and stamp the potato design. Use off-cuts of various sizes to stamp between the large images.

Layered stamping

Multiple stamping creates more interest and texture than simple stamping and works best with harmonizing colours. We used this technique on the tray on page 30 and the gift box on page 97.

1. Prepare or choose a background paper and various related images to layer, and assign harmonizing colours to the images. Ink your first image and complete its stamping. Allow the ink to dry before over-stamping with the next image or colour. Use a hairdryer to speed up the process.

2. Build up a layered look using transparent based light and dark inks. Add opaque and pearly or metallic inks for a richly textured result.

We used painted paper with diagonal drag textured lines and printed over with different leaves. The secret is knowing when it's enough. It's all about balance.

39

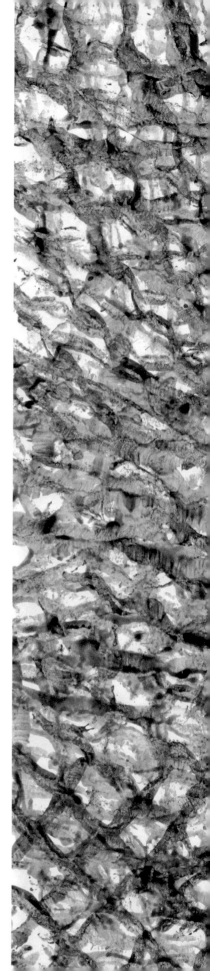

Reverse stamping

Also called stamping off, this is done by lifting wet paint off the surface to reveal a lighter impression. It works best on paper undercoated with extender or glaze. The images smudge easily as the paper surface is slippery – but this adds artistic charm! Painting large sheets of paper with fabric paint and using this technique creates lots of gift wrap very quickly. We layered our reverse stamping for more depth.

1 Coat paper with a layer of glaze or extender and wait a few minutes for the paper to absorb the coating. Sponge off excess if necessary. Ink over the coated paper with the chosen colour.

2 While this is still wet, impress with a clean, dry stamp. Lift off the ink revealing a lighter image on the inked surface.

3 Wipe the stamp clean and repeat or use a second stamp.

Modified stamping

For this you need a simple main stamp and several patterned stamps – bought foam ones work best with acrylic paint. We suggest this as a way to jazz up plain large stamps that you have grown tired of using. The permutations and possibilities are endless. This technique is particularly effective for cards.

1 Modify a ready-inked, large foam stamp by stamping onto it with a smaller, patterned stamp with opaque white for best effect.

2 Stamp the modified image onto prepared paper.

3 Repeat, using a different stamp to modify your main stamp.

We used several images stamped onto ready-inked shell stamps. For interesting variations, try stamping with variegated colours or simply stamp ink off your prepared stamp.

Found objects

These are everyday items identified with a stamper's eye – get yours focused! Packaging foam and webbing, varnished egg boxes and other bits of cardboard and containers create interesting textures and patterns when stamped. Building up layers of textured stamping in harmonious colours creates richness and adds depth to any patterned paper. The more you over stamp the more the images merge to create different textures. If you feel your result is too messy, wait for the paper to dry and use as a background to begin the process again – using opaque and metallic paints which will stand out more.

1 Ink your chosen stamping surface by either tapping it onto a stamp pad or tapping an inked sponge onto it if it is large.

2 Press the stamping surface repeatedly onto the paper in many directions to build up texture.

41

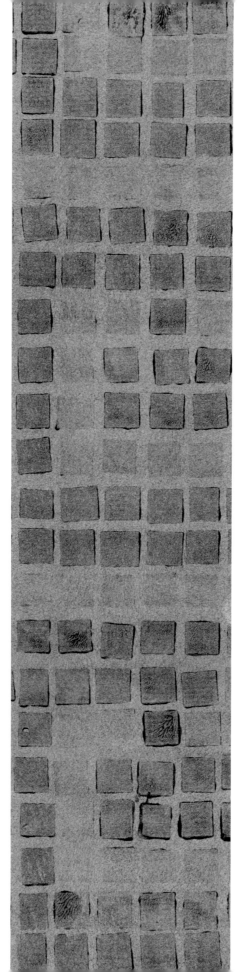

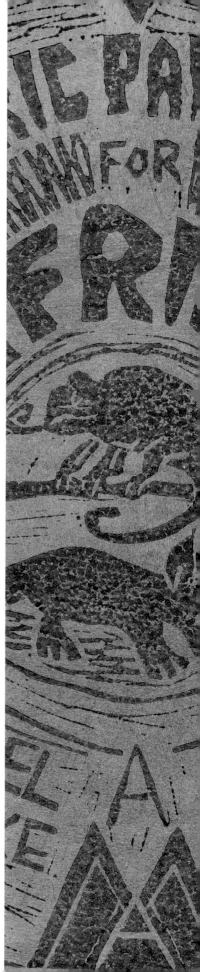

Home-made stamps

Your kitchen cupboards will produce a wealth of inspiration for making your own stamps. We used string glued to a support in different patterns to create the stamps for our paper.

1 Use strong, water-resistant, all-purpose adhesive to glue your stamp image to a support large enough to hold it. Stamp or draw the image on top as a direction indicator.

2 Ink and stamp as for ordinary stamping.

3 Repeat in combination with a similar-themed stamp.

Make your own stamps by drawing onto high density foam (recycle an old mouse-pad) with a dry ball-point pen. Cut around image and affix to a block. This can also be heated until it expands and then be impressed with an embossed or raised surface object which will leave a reversed impression.

Printing-block mosaic

Page-sized stamps or printing blocks are constructed in the same way as conventional stamps by glueing cut foam or a carved image to a large block. We used small cut squares for ours. Because of their size it is sometimes easier to apply the paper to the printing block rather than the other way round as in ordinary stamping. Rolling over the paper with a brayer results in an even print.

1 Ink a large mosaic stamp-board in a pattern with a paintbrush. If you are using more than one colour, add at this stage. Some inks and paints dry quickly, so we recommend slower-drying fabric paint if you are using more than one colour.

2 Print by laying a sheet of paper onto the inked mosaic board and rolling with a brayer. Carefully remove the printed copy to avoid smudging the pattern.

Lino-block printing

The example we have included here is a very crude first attempt by Angie as a cover for our original Fabric Painting for Africa manual which we produced ourselves! It's now quite a joke – spot the errors – but an image of our past. Lino has an irregular charm to it and lino prints make excellent book covers and illustrations, posters, cards and pictures. Smaller lino stamps are long lasting and offer a handmade alternative to conventional rubber stamps.

1 Carve lino using lino cut tools. Heating the lino first in a slow oven, or with a hairdryer while you work will make it easier to carve. Glue the carved piece to a solid piece of wood the same size.

2 Ink the lino block evenly using a sponge roller.

3 Print by laying the paper over the lino block and rolling over the paper with a brayer.

Stencilling

A stencil is a shape punched or cut out of card or plastic and, as with stamping, is a quick method of repeating a design. Simple and easy to use, bought stencils come in a variety of sizes and designs and are available from craft, hardware or paint shops. There are many creative possibilities for making your own stencils too — from drawing around your hand on an old X-ray and cutting that out, to painting around leaves from the garden to decorate a sheet of wrapping paper. Stencils can be positive (when you paint inside the shape) or negative (when you paint around the shape and use it as a block out). In this section we demonstrate both techniques.

Opposite page and right: No paper book would be complete without lots of paper planes! We doled out decorated paper to various friends and school children, who had enormous fun folding and flying paper planes of many shapes and sizes. As with the pinwheels on page 69, our ideas were a tad extravagant. We had 200-odd planes made, but had forgotten the logistics of flying them. While they didn't need aviation fuel, the helium balloons purchased to float them, did not have a fraction of the lifting power we thought they would have. Even doubling our original estimate did not come close. We eventually chose the 24 lightest planes and launched them aloft. (Thanks for the aeronautical tip, Liz!) The planes display various decorative techniques from scraping, mosaic block printing and stamping, to dip dyeing and dry brushing. You have probably spotted several more!

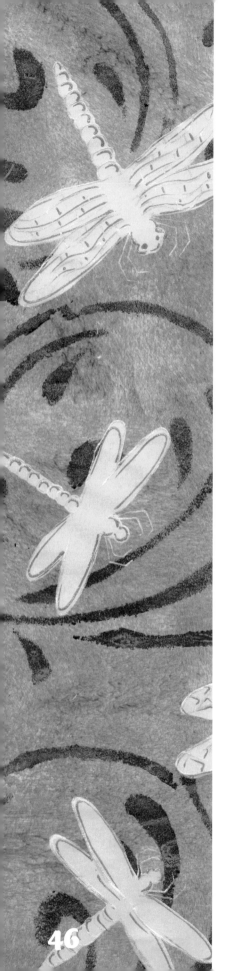

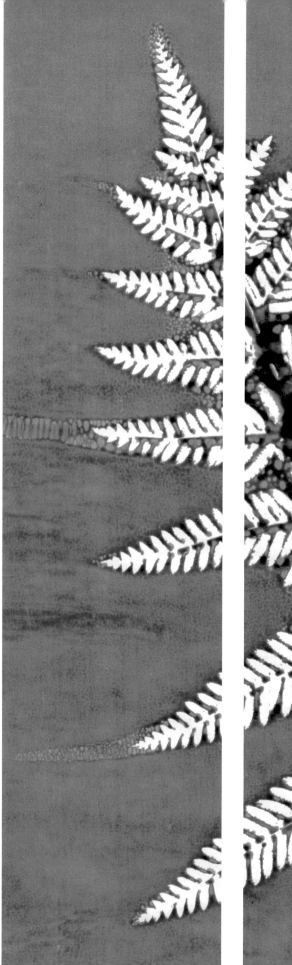

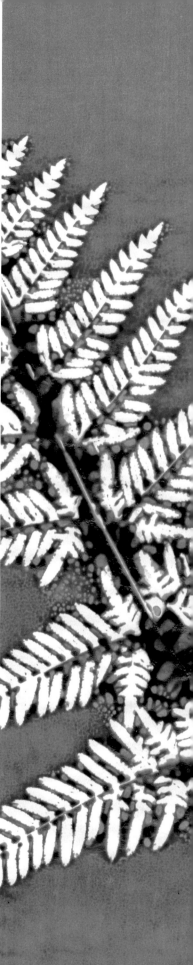

Hand-made block-out

A block-out is a solid shape which is cut out and used as a negative stencil or mask – the area around it is painted. These are very easy to make yourself and add a quirky touch to any scrap-book page or card.

1 Cut dragonfly (or other shapes) out of old X-rays or contact paper and place them in position on your paper. Apply paint over the entire piece of paper.

2 Leave as is or add a simple stencil as texture in the background.

3 Remove the masks and add detail with a milky pen.

Use coloured paper or apply a wash to the background beforehand if you do not want the shapes to be white. We applied a light blue wash to the paper, and finished the dragonflies with different patterns in silver and blue milky pens.

Screen-printing

The most accurate way to use flat, natural objects as stencils, is to screen print them. This is a good introduction to the art of screen-printing of which we will only touch on the basics here. If you don't have a bought silk-screen, make one from nylon mesh or fine net curtaining stapled to a frame. You may have to do several prints before you perfect the technique, but it becomes an addictive exercise and you'll have some wonderful paper pieces to show for it. We used a pressed fern leaf for this example.

1 Find flat leaves and press them in an old telephone book or iron them between sheets of paper if you are in a hurry.

2 Prepare a printing surface which has some give: layers of newspaper covered with a piece of thin foam sponge or thick fabric. Cover with plastic and finally position a sheet of paper (bigger than your required print size) on it ready for printing.

3 Place the leaf you will be using as a stencil in position on the paper. Cover the surface with the screen, mesh side down in contact with the stencil and the paper.

4 Spoon fabric paint or printing ink right across the width of one end of the screen.

5 While holding the screen firmly onto the surface (it helps to have extra hands) pull the ink across the surface with a squeegee (or credit card if you are using a small screen) pressing it downwards as you go.

6 Lift the screen carefully. The stencil should have stuck to the screen with the paint, leaving the negative image on the paper.

Try printing grasses and fine flowers (small, fragile weeds work best). The contrast of dark-coloured inks makes the most dramatic negative prints. Paper cut-outs and doilies also make wonderful stencils for screen-printing. When you have finished printing, wash your screen before the ink dries in the mesh. If you are interrupted while printing, pull ink thickly across the mesh and leave it in position – this way it won't dry and clog the mesh. When you resume printing, re-pull the ink and continue the process.

Variegated stencilling

This is a simple stencil painted in various colours from light to dark. A blue wash was applied to the paper beforehand and it was allowed to dry before the stencils were painted in. This technique makes great border patterns for boxes and gift bags as well as paper friezes for pasting on walls.

1 Place the stencil in position and sponge in the lightest colour.

2 While still wet, sponge in a slightly darker colour, though cover less of the shape.

3 Repeat with the darkest colour and lift stencil without smudging paint.

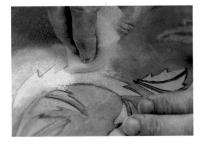

We used white, medium blue and dark blue for our leaves on an already painted background.

Colour separation

More complex, or multiple stencils, may need a separate stencil for each colour, and are laid onto the paper and painted one after the other so that the image is built up. As with variegated stencilling, this technique can be used for gift wrap, designs on boxes and other larger décor items.

1 Place the stencil for the lightest colour in position and sponge the colour in. It is usually advisable to leave the first colour to dry before applying the next, as this prevents smudging.

2 Place the stencil for the second colour in position and sponge in.

3 Repeat with the darkest colour. Remove the stencil, allow to dry and add detail with a pen.

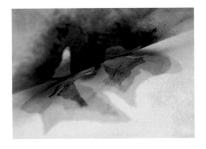

We used a silver milky pen to add veins to our ivy leaves stencilled in several shades of blue.

Shadow stencilling

This technique makes use of a negative stencil and creates a sense of depth. The secret is knowing when to stop, so don't overdo it. It is advisable to use absorbent paper such as water-colour paper, since more paint is used than usual. As water-colour paper is quite expensive, this technique would be best used for unusual scrapbooking pages or cards for really special people!

1 Colour your paper with a wash and leave to dry.

2 Place the stencil shape in position and sponge around it, creating a shadow and leaving a lighter shape underneath.

3 Move the stencil and repeat in the new position, though not over the previous image.

4 Continue in this fashion until the page is as full as you wish it to be, but don't overdo it.

Resists

Any medium other than stencils that is used to mask areas from paint is called a resist. Stencils, which have already been dealt with, are a variation of resists. Stencils mask out areas completely, while resists allow paint to seep through to varying degrees, often creating a less solid mask than a stencil. Resists also add texture to a page, often creating a three-dimensional appearance. Several mediums can be usedas resists, as shown on the following pages.

Right: With beaded curtains making a comeback, I thought it would be nice to do one in paper. Vellum decorated with blue, turquoise and a little yellow and pink glass paint was the perfect option. I didn't want a definite design and created a watery effect by streaking the vellum with paint, adding the accent colour here and there, and then spraying with methylated spirits and water which made the paint move, leaving circles, like ripples on the water in a pond when you throw a stone into it. I repeated the process on the reverse side, which created a double image and made the effect more interesting. For strength, the vellum was laminated and then cut into diamond shapes. These were strung together through small holes made at the top and bottom of each diamond, using gut and crimps. The strings of diamonds were then threaded onto an aluminium rod to form the curtain – the movement made by the breeze completed the watery effect (also see photograph on page 5).

Opposite page: When receiving take-home food in a box like this from one of the larger coffee shops on my beat, I thought that it would look very nice painted – I couldn't have a white box in the house! After painting one, I decided that a whole group would look even better. As the finish on the boxes is a glossy one, I used a watery effect. Cold glue was used to stamp circles and shells onto the boxes and when dry, I washed on very liquid acrylic paint and sprayed with water. While this was still wet, I sprinkled on some coarse salt which added to the texture. Imagine your guests' faces at your next dinner party when you serve Chinese stir-fry in these – just don't forget the chopsticks!

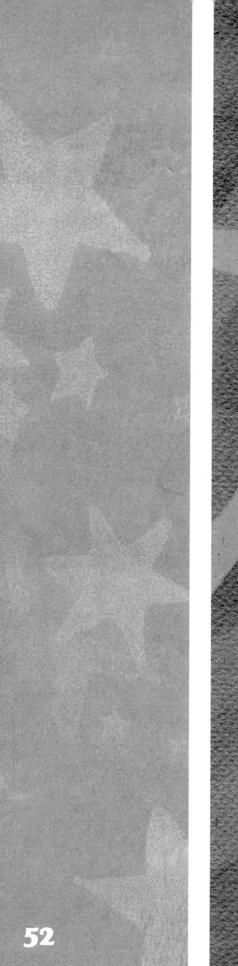
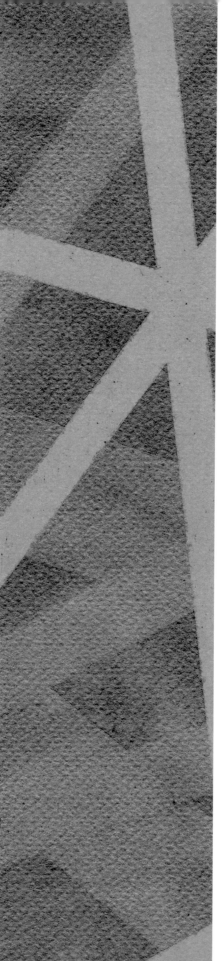
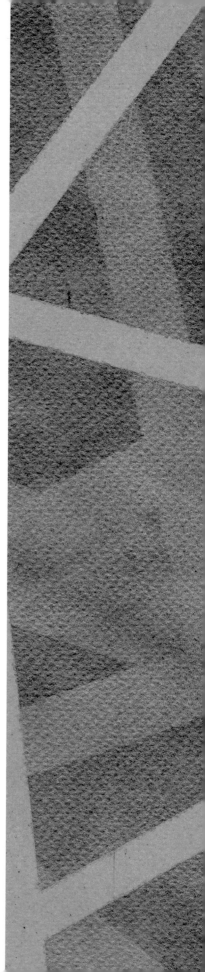

Extender

Fabric paint extender is a clear acrylic base which acts as a barrier to acrylic inks and water-diluted paints. The effect is noticeable but quite subtle. A clear stamp pad also works well as a resist medium. This has been used for a very subtle effect on the quaint pair of shoes on page 20.

1 Stamp the paper with images inked with extender. We used stars of various sizes. Leave for a few minutes so that the paper can absorb the extender.

2 Cover the paper in colour, over the extender, using a roller, sponge or paintbrush. The stamped sections will appear lighter than the rest of the paper. The effect intensifies as the paint dries.

Masking tape

Use masking tape as a resist for sharply defined, straight lines. Create a layered effect with successive colours and layers of masking tape criss-crossing to form interesting angles and shapes.

1 Low-tack masking tape strips by pressing them onto a fabric surface. They will pick up a fine layer of fibres thereby reducing stickiness. It is important to do this before laying the tape strips onto paper otherwise they will tear the paper when you lift them.

2 Lay tapes criss-cross onto paper leaving interesting spaces between the angles.

3 Paint over the tapes and allow to dry well.

4 Lay more tape strips over existing ones – try using different widths of tape. Paint over the paper again in a darker transparent colour. Allow to dry well and repeat for further depth if necessary.

5 Remove the tapes carefully by pulling back gently.

If masking tape does threaten to tear the paper, wait until the paint effect is dry and moisten the tape carefully with water, wait for it to be absorbed and then lift the tape gently.

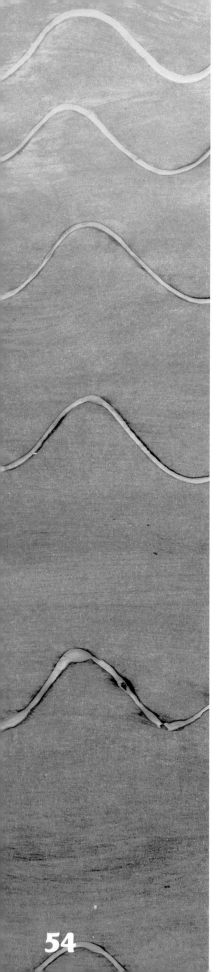

54

Starch or wood glue

This is a resist which adds texture to your page as well as interesting colour variations. We used this technique to add an extra texture to the Chinese take away boxes on page 51.

1 Make up a cooked starch mixture – as for paste painting (see page 104) or use wood glue straight from the nozzled bottle to draw wavy lines across the paper.

2 For a blurred effect, paint over the lines before dry.

3 For a more subtle result, allow the lines to dry and then over-paint. This will give shiny texture over starched lines, while wood glue resists paint much more and appears clear.

Colours and resist can be further layered as for the batik technique (see pages 60-61) and the latex technique discussed next.

Simple latex

Water-colour artists use latex to mask and layer sharply defined free-form resists in their painting. It is ammonia based, has a strong smell and is fairly expensive. Clean brushes with mineral turpentine when dry.

1 Paint liquid latex onto paper with a brush. This dries almost instantly to a yellow rubbery layer. We painted spots and flicked even smaller dots off an old toothbrush to represent stars in a night sky.

2 Paint over the latex with any water-based medium. Allow to dry.

3 Rub off latex spots with fingers when dry. If stubborn spots refuse to lift, rub gently with an eraser.

A variation of this starry sky was used for the wine label In Vino Veritas (see page 30).

Multi-layered latex

This works on the same principle as batik. Care should be taken with the choice of colours when using transparent paint or dyes, as each colour used will affect those added afterwards. The layering of colours is shown off particularly well when held up to light. We used this to good effect on our lanterns on the next page.

1 Paint the latex on the motifs which are to remain the colour of the paper.

2 Paint over the whole sheet with the first colour.

3 Leave the first layer of latex in place and add more latex to the motifs which are to remain the paint colour. Many layers of latex and paint can be added, though we have only used two in our example.

4 When the work is finally dry, rub away the latex to reveal all the colours and patterns used.

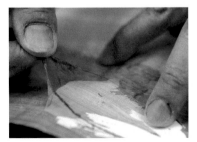

Wax & oil

Wax and oil can be used as further forms of resist or applied directly onto paper for their colours. Wax and oil coat paper with a protective, water-resistant layer. This can leave oily stains unless sealed with a protective coating or ironed between blotting papers to remove any excess. These mediums have been used since ancient times to bind pigments and in the following pages we have explored from the simplest to the more sophisticated applications.

Right: On this scrapbook page a photo frame was made with water-colour paper that had first been clouded, and while still wet, textured with clingfilm which was left in place until the paper was dry. The paper was cut in strips and wrapped around a cardboard frame. The torn paper in the background was decorated in the same way.

Opposite page: If you have a honey jar and a piece of A4 paper you can make a lantern. Add a wire handle and it will hang. The paper for these lanterns was patterned with the latex resist technique (see previous page) which is very effective for any kind of light, as the layering of paint allows different strengths of light to shine through. Burning the candles, held in place with sand, for a long time may damage the paper. This is simply a good excuse to paint more!

For an easy way to make the lanterns fit a standard honey jar, follow these cutting and folding instuctions: cut the paper to measure 21 x 28 cm. Lay the paper down horizontally, pattern side down. Fold one top corner over to meet the bottom edge and the other top corner down so the sides meet forming a 90°-angle. Crease the fold lines. Open the paper out and repeat for all four corners. Open out and place horizontally again. Next, fold the two top corners in, towards each other, until they meet at the centre. Crease the fold lines. Open out and repeat with the two bottom corners. A perfect diamond grid will have formed. Turn the paper over, pattern side up, and fold in half with the two long sides together. Unfold. Repeat folding and unfolding, each time meeting the previous fold line, until you have five parallel lines crossing the diamond intersections. Bend the paper round to form a cylinder, joining the two short ends on the inside with tape – the diagonal folds will pop out. Slide this over your honey jar and you're ready for a party.

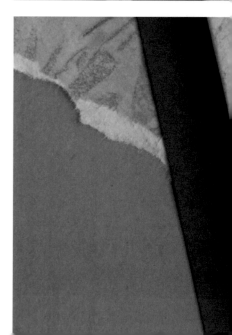

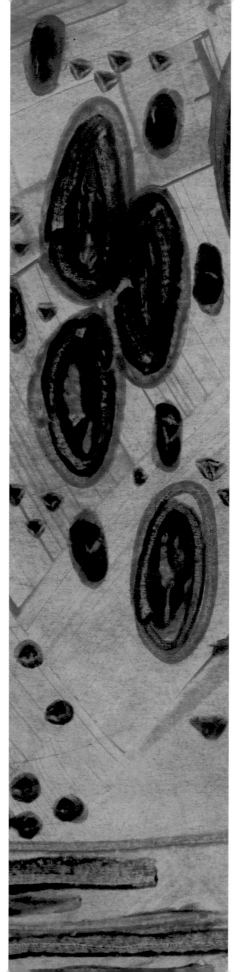

Grated crayons

Creating a speckled effect with wax crayons is really easy. Use recycled paper and the end bits of crayons that are too short to be used for any other purpose and you can also feel good about doing your bit for the environment. A variation to try with children is to allow them to sharpen wax crayons onto a piece of paper. An adult should use the iron to melt the wax. The resulting mixture of colours would work well for torn papers in a collage.

1 Grate the crayons onto paper, using a fine grater. This is a bit messy, so protect your work surface. Distribute over the entire paper surface.

2 Place a clean piece of paper on top and iron. You will be left with a speckled effect on both sheets.

The density will depend on the amount of crayon you have grated. Don't use too many colours, as this may become very messy.

Encaustic art

Encaustic art uses special wax crayons (beeswax and pigment) and heat. An encaustic iron (smaller than your home iron and certainly not with steam holes) is sometimes used where the wax is melted on the iron and applied to the paper to form interesting patterns and pictures. The wax can also be heated and painted on with a brush or hot palette knife. Encaustic wax will melt quicker and dry shinier than ordinary wax crayons. We used a hot tray for our version of encaustic art.

1 Place a sheet of paper onto a larger protective sheet on the hot tray and allow to heat through. Apply wax crayons as a background and scrape over the page with a credit card to create texture.

2 Draw your design with the wax crayons. The wax will melt and the different colours will merge. The pattern can be changed as long as the paper remains warm.

Sgraffito

This refers to a technique where one layer of colour is scraped off to reveal another layer underneath. Wax forms a soft layer on paper and can be scratched away to reveal any underlying colours. You can rub oil pastels over wax crayon patterns and scratch through to reveal multi-coloured patterns. Craft paint can also be used as a top layer. A favourite variation of this with young artists is to block over bright, waxy pictures with black crayon and then scrape away a picture.

1 Draw patterns with wax crayons onto paper. Cover the wax patterns with a thick layer of oil pastel in a dark colour. This may not necessarily block out some darker colours used in the underlying pattern.

2 Use a toothpick, bamboo skewer and your finger nail to scratch patterns into the pastel coating and reveal the underlying colours. Seal with clear lacquer spray.

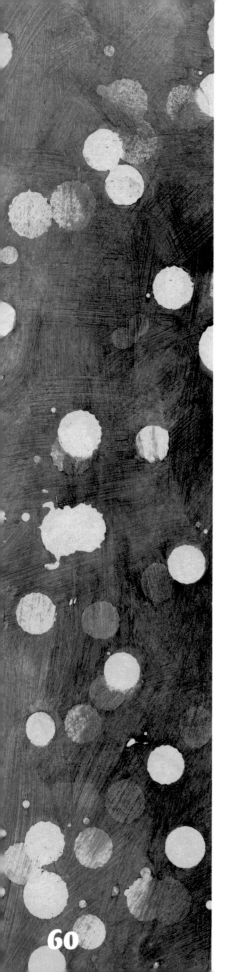

60

Simple batik

Alternating patterns and layers of melted wax and inks or dyes may be applied to paper in the same way as for cloth batik. We have included a much simpler form for the more decorative purposes of this book, which could be used to make a strong gift bag for food items such as biscuits which may leave oily marks on ordinary paper.

1 Melt and drop candle wax randomly on paper.

2 Cover the paper and wax dots with a transparent colour wash.

3 When the paper is dry, further wax drops and washes can be applied and added in layers until the desired effect is achieved.

4 Iron the paper between sheets of clean paper to absorb the wax.

Traditional batik

This fish design is done like traditional batik, which is quite a process. It requires a good understanding of colour mixing besides the technicalities of melting and applying wax. A wax mixture containing mostly paraffin wax, with a little beeswax to bind it will result in a heavy crackle effect. (Paraffin wax alone will flake off as you brush the dye on the paper.) For a more flexible finish, resulting in little or no crackle, increase the proportion of beeswax. Follow the steps to create this particular paper and then experiment further if the technique appeals to you.

1 Draw the fish design outlines lightly in pencil or chalk on light green paper.

2 Paint hot melted wax with a bristle brush all over the paper except in the fish designs.

3 Crumple the paper slightly and sponge it all over with medium green fabric paint. Allow to dry – do not apply heat to dry as the wax will melt.

4 Re-apply wax partially over the paper and particularly on the now medium green painted fish bodies with a thin brush to form fine lines depicting scales, rings around the eyes and fins. Crumple the paper again slightly.

5 Sponge dark blue-green paint over the paper – as this is the last paint layer you may dry the paper now with a hairdryer if you are in a hurry.

6 Iron the batik between two clean sheets of paper to absorb the wax and flatten the paper.

Wax stencilling

Instead of having to draw shapes freehand, it's easy to crayon through a simple stencil, especially if you want a repetitive design. The result is quite crude but effective, particularly when washed over with diluted colour. This could keep children busy for hours!

1 Draw with crayon through stencils, filling the shapes. Use simple stencil shapes without too many fine lines into which the crayon points won't fit. Use more than one colour for interest.

2 Apply a wash over the waxed motifs using paints in various shades of the same hue, or harmonious colours for an interesting effect.

You can also paint melted wax through stencils with a small, stiff-bristled (natural fibre) brush you don't mind messing up. This is another form of batik and the images can be over-painted in the same way.

White wax

A simple white wax candle can also be put to good use to decorate paper.

1 Use an ordinary white wax candle to draw lines onto paper. Wash over with transparent based yellow acrylic or water-colour paints to reveal the pattern.

2 Draw more candle lines over the yellow wash when dry and apply a transparent blue wash over the paper. The yellow and white lines will resist the blue wash and the yellow wash will turn green as seen through the transparent blue wash.

3 Create layers of colours in the same way as for batik.

You can try more complicated patterns and experiment with colour combinations. Or use wax crayons in harmonizing colours to draw patterns on paper and apply a wash over to create a similar effect.

Wax solvents

Turpentine is a solvent for oil-based paints and pastels. Oil washes created by diluting oil paint with turpentine impart a wonderful translucent colouring and waxy finish to ordinary copy paper. Wax crayons and oil pastels dissolve in white spirits or mineral turpentine. A simple scratchy crayon picture can be turned into something out of the ordinary by washing it like this.

1 Scribble a pattern in oil pastels in an harmonious colour range on paper.

2 Use a cheap oil-paintbrush dipped into turpentine to wash across the patterns. The oil colours will dissolve and blend to form a lovely, translucent waxy pattern.

Once this surface is dry, you could draw onto it with pens or kokis to define more detailed patterns – the waxiness of the paper will not resist them. We drew a simple wave pattern in sea greens and blues.

63

Checks & stripes

Checks and stripes are very simple to create on paper and there are various methods. The simplest way to paint checks is to paint a series of parallel stripes, and then to paint crosswise over them another series of parallel stripes in transparent-based paint. Vary the width of the stripes for an interesting effect, as we have done in this section.

Right: A collection of papier-mâché bowls decorated with various paint techniques. The bowls were all coated with several layers of either gloss or matt varnish to seal and protect them. Xoli's green bowl on the left has moulded papier-mâché fruit on the outside, dry brushed with a lighter green craft paint to show off the fruits in relief. Gemma pasted the middle bowl with pale green, blue and yellow postage-stamp sized paper pieces, over-painted with transparent cyan fabric paint inside and green outside, which allows the original paper colours to show as different tones of blue and green.

The shallow green bowl was painted with various shades of blue and green craft paint, and decorated with spotted leaf designs and concentric dot patterns in black, white and yellow. Rae painted the large polka-dot bowl with plain lime PVA. The polka dots are different sizes in blue, white and yellow acrylic colours with further details in white milky pen. The bowl was sealed with clear lacquer spray. The remaining bowl (see close-up **top right**) was decorated with overlapping triangular scraps of various painted papers in harmonizing colours and decorative techniques, with the brown-paper papier-mâché showing through.

Elizabeth Louise covered the styrofoam monkey balls with triangular paper pieces pasted with wall-paper glue.

If papier-mâché bowls are to be used and washed they should be coated with at least three layers of linseed oil and baked between coatings. This discolours them somewhat, but renders them effectively waterproof.

Bottom right: On this scrapbook page the fresh colours of the woven strips of faux marbled paper in blue, and green paper textured with bleach granules complement the photos and each other. The darker turquoise paper was painted with dark blue fabric paint and scraped.

Opposite page: The striking colours on this handmade sisal bowl come from lime green and blue sun paint. We wet a large sheet of sisal paper, draped it over a large ceramic bowl and moulded it by hand with wallpaper paste to the contours of the bowl. The edges were torn and frayed to fit and the bowl baked in a slow oven to dry for a few hours. Before removing it from the ceramic bowl we applied two layers of matt epoxy varnish to the outside for strength.

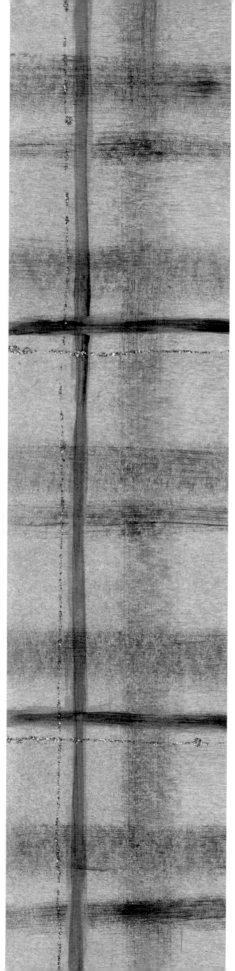

Brushed stripes

When painting thick lines it is best to use brushes which have longer, slightly floppy bristles for dragging.

1 Use different widths of brushes with different colours to make slightly uneven drag-textured stripes across a page, leaving gaps between.

2 Fill in more stripes between these and allow to dry.

3 Add interest by drawing thinner lines with a wax crayon and a milky pen on top of the painted stripes.

While dragging, the trick is not to load the brush too heavily as the paint will squeeze out at the sides of the bristles and leave thicker blobs of colour which can smudge easily.

Dry-brushed tartan

Dry-brushing lines in various check and striped patterns has a unique effect. Combine it with a little glitter glue for festive wrapping paper.

1 Pick up a small amount of paint on a brush and paint it onto a palette to work the paint into the bristles before applying it to the paper. Drag the paint brush across the paper to make soft, lightly textured stripes and checks. The lines should be scratchy and a little patchy and can be built up by repeated dragging of the dry brush.

2 Dry-brush further lines using a slightly thinner brush.

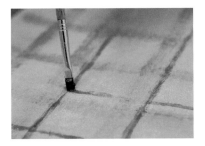

Finish off by adding lines in glitter glue, ensuring that an even pressure is applied to avoid blobs.

Roller checks

There are so many interesting rollers available. Some have holes or slices cut in them, others a rough textured foam for different effects. Try wrapping string or elastic bands around your rollers before inking them to create different stripes. Put a few different coloured inks or paints onto a palette before inking with the roller to get vari-egated stripes!

1 Roll interesting textured lines of colour with a small sponge roller to make quick stripes.

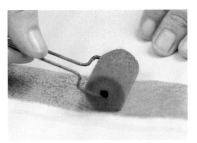

2 Make sure the first row of stripes is dry before rolling over them crosswise to form checks. This will prevent smudging and blending of colours.

3 Add further interest with wide lines using a patterned roller.

Wet work

With most of the techniques discussed on the following pages we worked with very liquid or watered-down paints on wet (or dry) paper. Paper stretches when wet and will buckle as it dries. To prevent this from happening, you can pre-stretch the paper or use a heavy quality water colour paper. If using ordinary copy paper place it under heavy weights when dry or iron on the wrong side to flatten.

To pre-stretch paper, wet it with a sponge and place flat on a Masonite board. Tape the edge of the paper onto the surface with sticky brown paper tape. Allow the paper to dry. Work your technique onto the paper and allow it to dry again before cutting it free from the brown paper tape lines with a craft knife.

Top right: Sarie made this colourful posy from the smallest scraps of faux textured papers mounted on bleach discharged green paper, all in striking contrast with the dark blue cardstock.

Right: An abstract collage of cut and torn cracked-paint paper interleaved with red mirror-printed scraps stuck onto gold and brown dragged papers. The white card background shows off the white torn edges of the scraps.

Bottom right: The blue card in the background has a seashell fastened to a scrap of thin cork matting, framed by a piece of paper decorated with mosaic-board stamping. On its left is Debbie's card from our range of yellow and red marbling (see pages 110-113) mounted on red spun-bond paper. The heart on the black card was cut from white paper partially painted with red PVA. A scribbly outline with a white milky pen lifts it off the background.

Opposite page: We imagined an entire field of bright pinwheels spinning their colours in the wind. But after painting, varnishing and making 39 pinwheels, we were easily convinced that a clump would have to do! The solid colours of the pinwheels were brushed onto card and then varnished (thanks Lynne!) for strength, while the patterned papers were glued back-to-back to stiffen them. The techniques include wax and latex resist, marbling, beetroot paper, mosaic stamping, bleaching and scraped patterns.

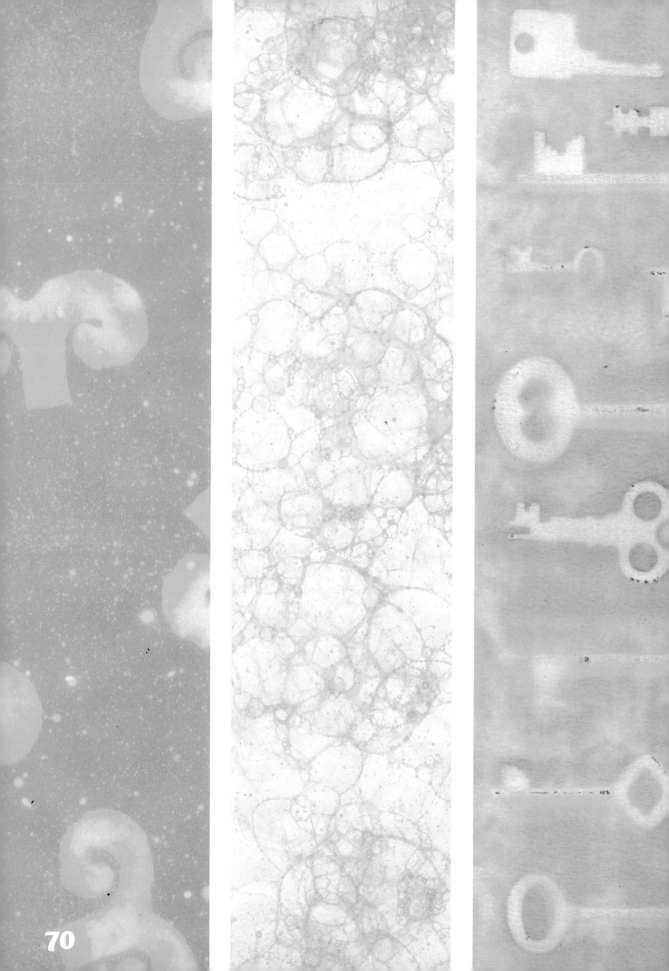

Bleach patterns

Mediums that remove or discharge colour from paper can be used quite effectively to decorate paper and create interesting effects. See the lime green paper used for a weave pattern in the scrapbooking page 64.

1 Paint, spray or stipple thick bleach onto absorbent coloured papers to discharge the original dye colour of the paper.

2 Wait until a stipple or spatter pattern appears on the paper and overstamp with simple stamps using thick bleach.

Try wetting the paper before dropping or painting with bleach for a washed out effect. Sprinkle wet coloured paper with chlorine granules for a reverse 'salt technique' and try painting designs in thickened bleach for more distinctly controlled patterns.

Bubble prints

Create unusual bubble patterns on paper with a mixture of ink and liquid detergent. This is a fun activity for children, with the advantage that the detergent prevents the paint staining too radically. This technique works best using strong inks on dry copy paper.

1 Mix 1 part acrylic ink and 1 part liquid detergent in a small container such as a plastic cup.

2 Insert a straw and blow until bubbles pile up a few centimeters above the rim of the cup.

3 Gently place a sheet of paper onto the bubbles and lift off immediately. The bubbles will print themselves onto the paper surface. Repeat until the paper is covered.

Don't skimp on the detergent as your bubbles will be too light and burst too easily, spoiling the pattern. If this happens, add more detergent.

Sun paint

You need calm, sunny weather for this technique to work, using any flat, opaque object as a block out for printing. Stones, leaves, negative stencils, or other weighted, found objects act as stencil resists by allowing the paint to dry in darker patterns around them. I used a wonderful collection of keys – the older ones even left authentic rust marks to add to the charm. Use good quality water-colour paper for the best effect. This is a great technique to use for a 21st birthday card.

1 Wet paper thoroughly and blot between dishtowels. Sponge on sun or silk paint, or liquid pigment dye. Place flat objects or block-outs onto paper surface and leave in a clean, windless, sunny place until dry.

2 Remove the block-outs – the dyed areas exposed to the sun will be strongly coloured (suntanned!) and the parts under the block-outs will be lighter.

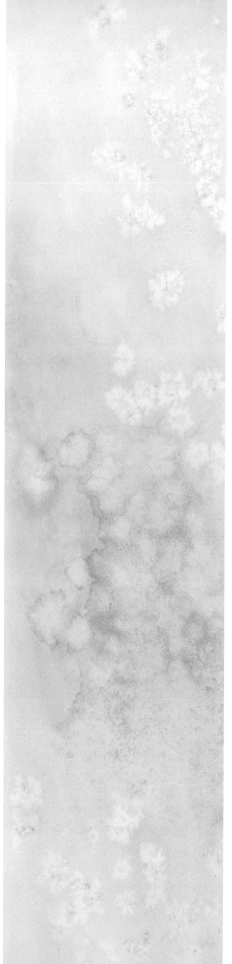

Salt-water paper

Salt is hygroscopic which means it absorbs moisture. Use this quality in combination with paint to create a crusty texture on paper. This makes lovely vegetation effects for landscape paintings or collages.

1 Paint a strong salt-water solution onto paper and allow it to dry.

2 Paint the paper with transparent acrylic inks and watch the paint run and bleed into the fine salted surface.

3 When dry, iron the paper on the wrong side and then brush the right side with a stiff brush to remove the loose salt from the surface. Some salt will remain, adding to the texture.

Salt-crystal speckling

Use the hygroscopic quality of salt for a granular effect. The salt is sprinkled over the paint, resulting in a speckled finish. This technique added lots of texture to the otherwise plain Chinese take-away boxes on page 51.

1 Ink or paint a piece of paper in one or several colours.

2 Sprinkle the wet paper with coarse, medium or fine salt crystals and allow to dry. The salt will absorb the moisture and draw the colours towards each crystal, drying in darker patches where the crystals touch the paper surface. This will result in a speckled, crusty texture depending on the size and quantity of salt crystals used.

3 Shake off any excess crystals when the paint is completely dry.

Try a variation by dropping salt and inks onto paper together.

Clouding

This technique works best on pre-stretched copy paper or good quality water-colour paper. Water-colour artists use it for sky in landscapes. Use it for a beautiful, gently blended effect on its own in just about any paper project. It makes a great background for stamping and printing over.

Wet the paper before softly rubbing colour onto the surface with a sponge or large, soft brush. A single colour or a number of analogous (harmonious) colours may be used.

2 Blend the colour while wet with a brush (a very soft hake brush made for this purpose works well.) Leave some areas softer and lighter for a clouded effect.

When a student asked me for my salmon brush, it took a detailed explanation before I realized Moira was after my hake brush. It's been known as the "fish and chips" brush ever since!

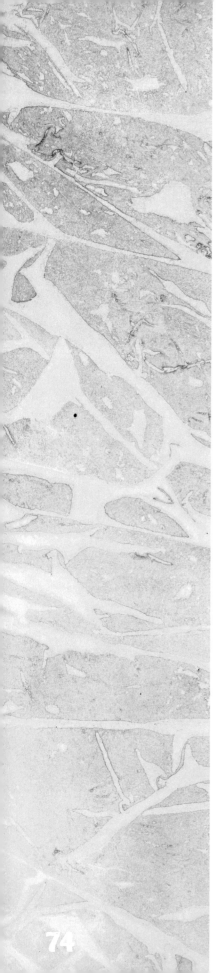

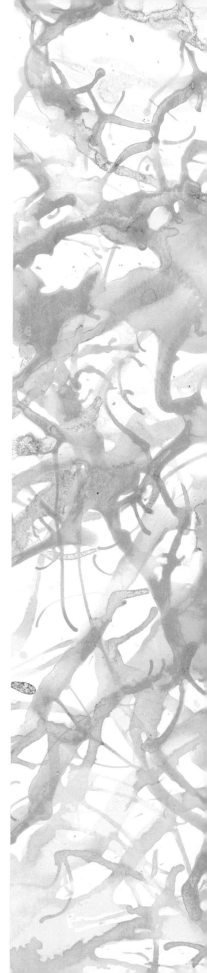

Cling-wrap creases

While this is essentially a wet technique, as the paper usually has to be wet before the colour is applied, fabric paint and paste paint work very well on dry paper too. This is also a great technique combined with brown ink or tea and coffee staining to create or enhance an aged look. We used this for added texture on our gift bag and gift wrap on pages 8 and 121.

1 Paint liquid dyes, inks or glazes onto paper until the surface is slick and quite wet.

2 Cover with creased plastic cling-wrap and leave to dry. This can take up to a few days depending on the weather. Do not be tempted to peek or rearrange cling-wrap until the paper is bone dry.

The resulting folds and pooling of dye between creases in the cling-wrap make a wonderfully textured design.

Dip dyeing

This resembles tie-dyeing on fabric and works best on soft, thin, dry paper which can be folded easily but yet unfolded again, without tearing, while still damp. The technique works well on tissue paper. Coloured paper dipped into bleach gives an interesting result. Jazz up plain paper napkins with this technique for your next dinner party.

1 Fold the paper into concertina pleats or cones. Dip the corners or edges into inks, dyes, bleach or liquid paints. Blot the wet paper on kitchen towel until just damp.

2 Leave for about 15 minutes for the ink to be absorbed and then unfold the paper very gently. If the paper doesn't unfold easily or threatens to tear, leave it a little longer before opening and pressing flat.

For extra effect, try re-folding the paper in another pattern and dipping into another colour.

Colour blowing

This technique works best on coated paper with a glossy finish. Very absorbent paper soaks the ink up too quickly for the right effect. Have several plastic straws handy. On glossy paper, this makes great little gift tags.

1 Dip straws into inks or very liquid paint and carefully suck a little up the straw – you don't want to swallow it!

2 Release the ink onto the paper with a sharp blow through the straw. Keep blowing the wet edges of the ink across the paper.

3 Repeat the process with further colours until you have a spidery effect of blown lines all over the paper.

Try plain black ink on white paper for dramatic effect – or variegated colours to simulate seaweed, like we've done for the example.

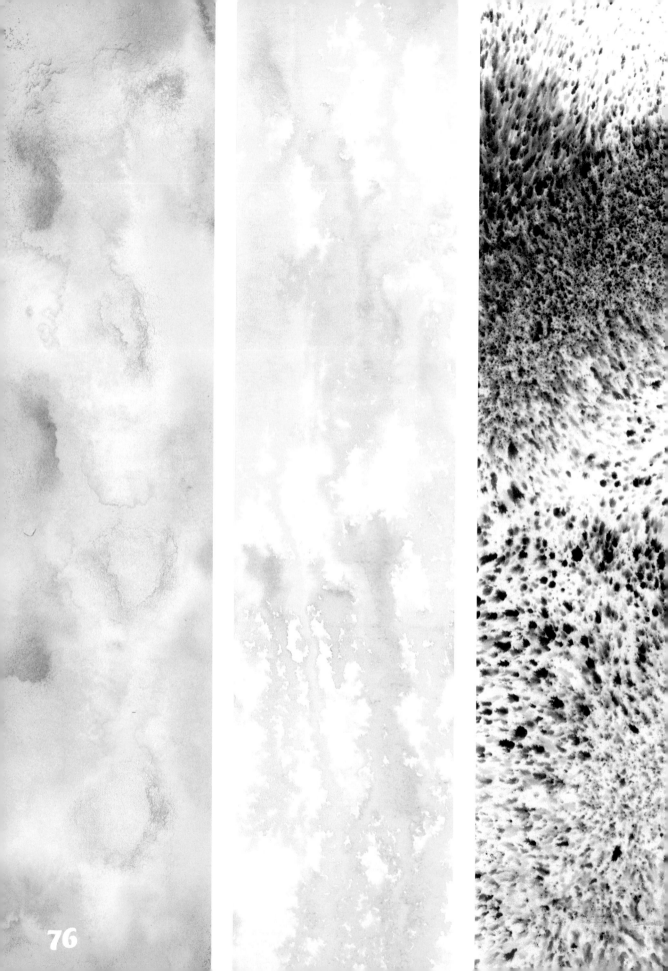

Dropped colour

When ink or paint is applied to wet paper it reacts in different ways depending on how it is applied. This gives you a lot of scope for decorating, and the same technique renders different results every time. Some of the kite papers (see page 109) were decorated like this.

1 Wet paper evenly with water from a spray bottle or sponge.

2 Drop coloured inks or diluted paints onto the surface. Allow to dry.

The inks or paints run and bleed and blend into each other and pool as the paper buckles while drying, never twice resulting in the same pattern.

Poured colour

This technique produces unique results with every attempt and is easy and effective. Apply the colours to a larger sheet of paper than you need and crop the section that works best. Use up left over paint in this way to make a supply of interesting and unusual colour combinations for collages. Sometimes the pouring results in an interesting picture of its own – so check it out before you cut it up!

1 Spray the paper with water or wet with a sponge.

2 Pour small pools of ink or paint onto one end of the paper – use two or three colours.

3 Hold the paper up so that the paint runs down. Once the colour has run down you can turn the paper so that the paint runs the other way, for a different effect. Dry flat.

Sprinkled colour

Many different colour pigments make up powder fabric dye. When used as a powder on wet paper, the different colours separate out, creating fascinating, almost three-dimensional effects. It is really messy, though, and can contaminate other projects, so it's best to work outside, away from your normal work area. This is one of Monique's favourite techniques. We used it for our logo and our wonderfully interesting beads.

1 Lay the paper flat and wet thoroughly with a sponge or brush.

2 Sprinkle the fabric dye onto the paper and watch the fabulous patterns appear.

3 The type of pattern will depend on the amount of dye sprinkled onto an area, so take care. Less is more!

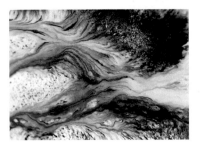

4 Seal this paper with clear lacquer spray or artists fixative to minimize contamination from excess powder.

Aged paper

Old papers made from wood fibres have a high acid content and deteriorate with age, becoming brittle, yellow and dotted with age spots. Try some of the following techniques to recreate an authentic antique or aged look. Aged paper is particularly effective for cardmaking and themed scrapbook pages.

Right: We have seen so many paper-bead projects that are very amateurish but Bernie has made a spectacular success of this necklace and bracelet. The combination of our paper beads with glass beads and crystals works really well. The paper beads are very easy to make by rolling triangles of decorated paper tightly around a toothpick. The width of the flat end of each triangle is about 2 cm while the length is that of an A4 piece of paper (21 cm). Any variation in width will affect the length of the bead. Start rolling at the base and glue the point to hold it in place. The paper we used was a similar piece to the sprinkled fabric-dye paper on the previous page. The finished beads were wiped over a clear stamp pad and embossed with transparent embossing powder. Some of the beads were lightly wiped over the stamp pad again and embossed with gold embossing powder as well for added sparkle. While time-consuming to make, these beads are really versatile and add a truly personal touch to any beading. Try making earrings as well.

Sacrament

Stamp-pad staining

A very easy, though less economic way of ageing paper is to stain it with bought stamp pads specifically made for this purpose. There are a number of colour variations available so the intensity of the aged effect will depend of the colour or combination that you use.

1 Spray a plastic sheet a little bigger than the paper with water, and wipe over this lightly with the stamp pad.

2 Lay your paper onto the wet plastic and smooth over. Lift the paper and allow to dry.

For a variation, soak paper in walnut ink and dry. Scrunch up quite tightly to create a very creased look. Smooth it out and lightly draw a stamp pad across the creases. The peaks will catch the colour of the pad. This effect can be softened by brushing with a little water. Iron the paper if you want it to lie flat.

Antique map

Your kitchen cupboards are a wonderful source of substances for ageing paper. Rather than show sheets of paper dyed with different types of tea and coffee we thought we'd create an antique-look map and jazz it up with some secret writing in lemon juice and burnt edges for a real treasure-map effect.

1 Paint or dip-dye copy paper with a strong solution of tea, Rooibos tea or coffee. Allow to dry – you can speed up the process in the oven or with a hairdryer but the paper will buckle. Oven drying will cause the paper to become quite brittle and it may crack when folded. This just adds an authentic antique touch!

2 Use calligraphy or mapping pens and strong black coffee to draw grid lines, direction arrows and features, such as a coastline on the map, as well as clues of a buried treasure, such as an eye and a flame.

3 Use a clean nib and lemon juice to write secret messages and directions you want to include on your map – we drew a cross, a wreck site (Sacramento) and dotted pathways and wrote place names.

4 Roll up the finished map and hold the rolled edges briefly in a candle flame to create burnt edges. Re-roll the opposite way and scorch those edges too. Rolling the brittle paper caused it to crack so we darkened the crack lines with more coffee and burnt them too for added effect.

The clues of the eye and the flame mean, "to see the secret message, apply heat". We've ironed this map to reveal the lemon juice writing which turns brown with heat.

By the way, the Sacramento was wrecked off our coastline in 1647. There was a real treasure and the map is reasonably accurate too. If you are ever in the Nelson Mandela Metropole in the Eastern Cape, find Schoenmakerskop and check it out. The treasure is in the museum, though!

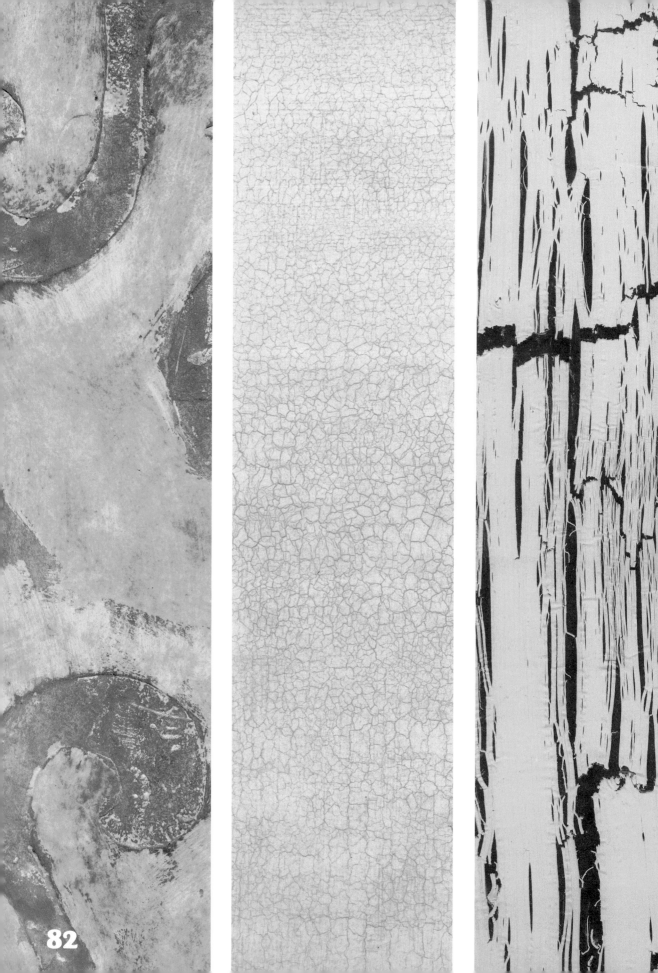

Crack filler & powder

Crack filler on paper will have a rough, raised surface like old plaster embossing. Some parts may flake off as it dries – this will add to the aged appearance. We used an example on a textured quick art block (see page 104-105) and left it unpainted for dramatic effect.

1 Paint paper with wood glue and shake powder (experiment with talc, scouring or crack-filler powder) over while the glue is still wet. Allow to dry and dry brush the whole page with sepia coloured acrylic paint.

2 Mix flexible crack filler with a little wood glue to improve adherence and brush, scrape, stamp or stencil it randomly over the powder-textured paper. We pasted it through the stencil with an ice-cream stick. Allow to dry.

3 Dry brush the raised stencilled shapes with acrylic paint when crack filler is dry.

Antique crackle

Fine porcelain-type crackle creates a cracked, distressed look on paper using the same crackle glazes as for decoupage techniques. This is a wonderful background paper for scrapbooking with old sepia coloured photographs or antique postcards.

1 Paint a layer of crackle base-coat onto paper. Allow to dry thoroughly and repeat.

2 When touch dry, apply crackle top-coat and wait for cracks to appear. This may take a few days to develop. Don't be tempted to use heat to speed up the process as the cracks must develop naturally. When you are happy with the amount of cracks, proceed to the next step.

3 Rub over cracks with burnt umber oil paint dissolved in a little turpentine. Leave for 5 minutes, wipe clean and buff gently for a lovely, aged finish. Seal with clear lacquer spray.

Cracked-paint effect

For large, random cracks use the sandwich type crackle glaze which is sandwiched between two layers of PVA. Or make your own glaze like we did. We used torn, cracked-paint paper to decorate the cat mask and cards – see pages 21 and 68.

1 Paint the paper with two coats of brown PVA and allow to dry. Paint a generous coat of wood glue over the brown PVA.

2 While the wood glue is still wet, paint a single layer of cream PVA carefully over it taking care not to overlap brushstrokes.

3 Large cracks will appear as the wood glue dries at a different rate to the overlying PVA thus pulling and stretching it apart into cracks. Once dry, the paper may be sealed with water-based varnish.

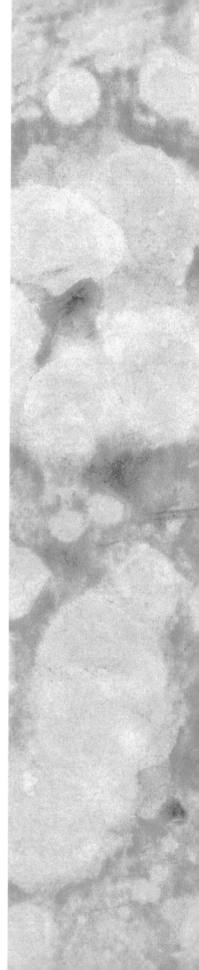

Shoe-polish ageing

The wax in shoe polish adds a smooth finish when buffed on any paper and neutral shoe polish can be used to seal absorbent paper. Coloured shoe polishes add tones to painted or printed papers and work particularly well on previously crumpled or folded paper as the shoe polish colours darken along the fold or crease lines resulting in an aged effect.

1 Crumple a sheet of paper (we first printed ours with an interesting rock painting font) and smooth it out onto the work surface.

2 Gently rub with any brown shoe polish and buff until the surface glows with a soft waxy sheen.

Mix polish colours randomly for a more interesting effect.

Sanded paper

This is a great way to use up reject papers from other decorating projects. Our sample was painted with two layers of brown PVA and allowed to dry before over-coating with cream PVA. The finished paper is thick and strong – use it for paper weaving, antique gift bags, or box or book covers.

1 Cover previously painted or decorated paper with two layers of cream PVA. Allow the paint to dry well after each coat. None of your undercoat colour will show through at this stage. Our sample shows the second coat of darker wet cream PVA over the light, dry first coat.

2 Sand the PVA layers carefully with a medium grit sandpaper until the base colour (brown) starts to show through.

Although PVA strengthens paper, always work gently with the sandpaper to avoid damage.

Solvent release

Water, mineral turpentine, methylated spirits and other solvents react in different ways when dropped or brushed on wet paint. The paint will begin to dissolve and move on the paper surface and if left to dry slowly will result in random, unpredictable patterns and textures. We dropped alcohol on scumble-glazed paper to create this effect on the red background paper for the backgammon board overleaf.

1 Combine 1 part acrylic scumble glaze (or glaze coat), 1 part water and 1 part paint to mix a glaze. Brush the glaze mixture onto paper.

2 Drop or spray a solvent over the painted paper while still wet.

3 Allow the solvent to push rings or lines into the glaze. Leave paper to develop and dry naturally or blow dry when you are happy with the effect. If it looks too flat, apply more glaze and solvent.

Faux finishes

Faux means fake. It is easy to simulate natural textural effects such as rock or wood graining with unusual tools and suitable colours. Texture adds interest to any project and is very important. It can be created in any number of different ways, most of which are really simple. We've adapted all sorts of techniques, including wall effects, for paper. The methods used here are all best executed using transparent based paints onto paper already coated with some form of transparent paint base or glaze. Fabric paint offers the most economical option and we've used it for most of these samples. If you are using PVA, mix a glaze in the ratio of 1 part scumble glaze to 1 part water to 1 part PVA.

Right: For these game boards we found two supawood boxes which just happened to be the right size. One exactly forms the lid, the other the base for a styrofoam casing of glass game pieces previously housed in a cardboard box. The paper for the chess board was painted as faux marble with pale green and grey fabric paint. The checks and borders were cut from paper bagged on with old metallic paint that was almost discarded out – it had gone black and rusty instead of gold and shiny. A little green and white PVA randomly stippled onto this gunge produced an authentic granite look.

The red base for the backgammon board was made lighter on one half by sponging one side of a previously folded sheet of paper with transparent scumble glaze. The other side was painted with red PVA thinned with scumble and then the two halves mirror-image printed (see pages 124-125). Denatured alcohol was sprinkled over the wet paint and allowed to form patterns on the surface. The dark green triangle markers and borders were cut from paper daubed and swirled with flat oil-paintbrushes and a mixture of black craft paint, green fabric paint and scumble glaze. The paper for the red triangles was sandwich printed (see pages 122-123) with red PVA dotted with black craft paint and small blobs of green fabric paint. The paper was decoupaged onto the boards with a mixture of wall-paper paste and wood glue and sealed with two layers of a matt epoxy floor varnish for strength.

88

Glas-marble rolling

With this technique you make random directional lines on pre-painted paper using glass marbles as a painting tool. The result is a texture similar to cross-grained schist (type of rock) or a close-up of matted fibres.

1 Stick paper to the base of a shallow baking or roasting pan with a few dots of sticky putty. Make sure there is plenty of space around the paper for some marbles and paint.

2 Pour a little liquid paint the consistency of thin cream along one edge of the pan. Pop marbles into the paint, tilt the pan and allow marbles to roll across the paper, trailing paint along the paper as they go.

3 Repeat with further colours until you are satisfied with the result.

Clean the marbles and wipe the previous colour off the pan before re-rolling the marbles.

Tortoiseshell effect

A tortoiseshell effect works best done in harmonious colours, either the traditional warm browns and oranges we have used here, or a different range altogether. Traditionally a paint technique used for furniture, it works well on covered boxes and other décor items such as photo frames.

1 Blob various glazes in browns, oranges, and a little black if you wish, across a page.

2 Daub the paint with brushstrokes diagonally across the page blending the glaze blobs.

3 Soften the tortoiseshell effect by lightly polishing the blended damp glaze with a hake brush.

Wood-grain effect

This is an easy technique requiring a special tool available from most hardware stores. It has semicircular grooves and leaves wood-knot patterns as it slides across glaze. We used this in blues and purples for the coasters and place mats on page 30.

1 Paint PVA glaze onto paper and while it is still wet, drag lines into the paint with a stiff bristled brush.

2 To complete the wood-grain effect with knotting as for heart-wood, rock a wood-graining tool across the wet glaze.

When my special wood-grainer disappeared after a workshop, I couldn't find another like it so I made my own by sticking concentric semicircles cut from sticky labels onto a piece of plastic gutter piping. It worked just as well until the sticky label paper got too wet and peeled off – but by then my project was done!

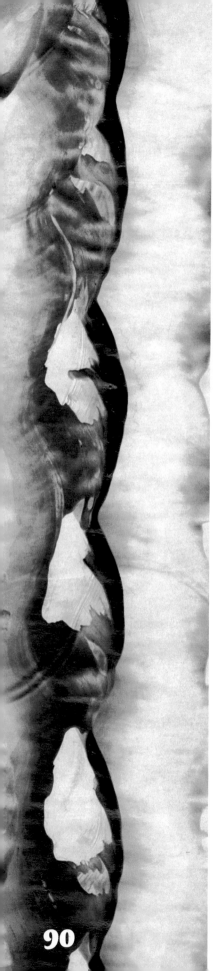

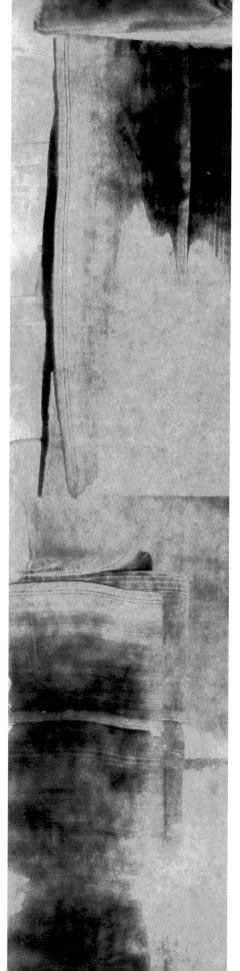

Cookie-cutter dragging

What an effective texture this is! It is really easy to achieve, but can be messy. For this reason it's advisable to use a piece of paper larger than you need and to crop away the edges. Use at most three harmonious colours. You could have great fun adding to any gift wrap selection with this technique.

1 Place the cookie cutter at one of the top corners of the paper and place a blob of each of your paint colours into the cutter.

2 Pressing firmly, drag the cutter across the paper in a straight line or waves, until you reach the other end. Pull down a little, ready for the next pattern.

3 Top up with blobs of colour, if needed, and repeat all the way down the paper. Don't wipe excess paint away as you will spoil the effect.

Card scraping

Card scraping is a very quick and economical method of applying paint over a large surface. Use a discarded credit card. Telephone cards also work well. This results in the bladed texture of rough stucco plaster. Any paint will work with this technique.

1 Scrape thin and uneven layers of paint onto paper in any direction, though we kept ours vertical and horizontal.

2 Repeat using different colours or shades. There is no need to allow the colours to dry in between applications. Leave interesting straight lines and edges if you use a transparent based paint such as fabric paint.

While any paint can be applied with a card to cover a surface quickly, the texture will show best if the paint is first mixed with a gel medium or extender. More colours can be blended in smoothly or added randomly as you go.

Bagging on

A scrunched up plastic bag can be used to take away or to apply paint. The effect will be subtly different. The kind of plastic you use will affect the finish. Traditionally used on walls, this technique is a fast way to cover a large surface and works well as a background paper for other techniques or on its own. Create a layered look for more depth by bagging with different colours. Allow the paints to dry between colours if you want a crisper finish. For a more subtle effect, blend the colours softly while wet.

1 Scrunch up a soft plastic bag and dab it into PVA glaze. Apply this in a random pattern to the paper.

2 Repeat the process using more colours if you wish.

We used brown paper. You can also apply a coat of paint to white copy paper before bagging on further colour.

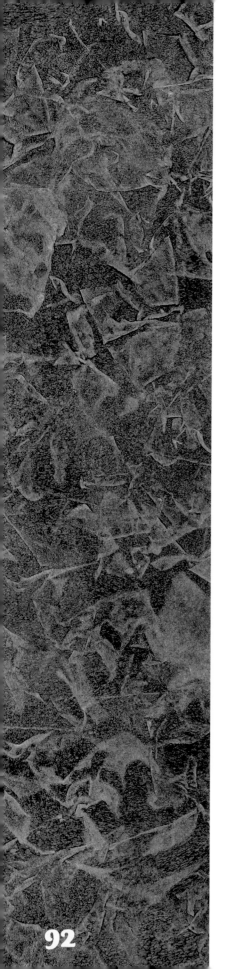

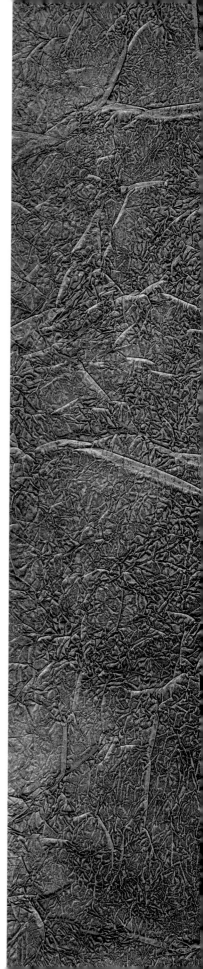

Scrunching off

Scrunched paper can be used just like a scrunched up plastic bag to apply colour or to take it off. Each different 'applicator' will have a different finish. This is a good way of recycling paper. If you are scrunching off, use the scrunched paper to stamp onto a clean piece of paper simultaneously to create different texture. Don't discard the scrunched up paper either, as it may offer interesting textured effects to add to collages or cards.

1 Paint PVA glaze mix onto paper (see page 85 for mixing ratios).

2 While still wet, lift glaze off by repeatedly dabbing with a ball of scrunched up paper – the result will resemble that of bagging off, though the marks will be more angular.

Paint blocks or stripes of different colours on your paper and allow to dry. Apply a glaze and scrunch off to reveal the different colours.

Granite finish

A sea sponge gives a lovely soft effect, but they are quite expensive and a crumpled piece of bubble wrap can be used if you do not have one. While we have chosen browns to fit into our colour theme, any combination of harmonious colours works well. A similar effect was used for the games on pages 85-97.

1 Use a sea sponge or crumpled piece of bubble wrap to tap a textured layer of paint onto paper.

2 Repeat the process with two progressively darker layers of sponging to form a close-grained granite texture.

3 Spatter black paint randomly with a toothbrush to finish off.

Old leather

Paper is a wonderful medium and with a bit of paint can be made to resemble just about anything. Here we used tissue paper to resemble worn leather.

1 Crumple a piece of tissue paper until is finely creased. Glue it down onto a sheet of paper or iron it onto a sheet of wax paper or the waxy backing paper from shelving contact. You can also stick it onto a sheet of clear contact.

2 We did not have brown tissue paper which is what we needed so this could fit in with our colour scheme. But we did have purple paper and orange paint, and the combination of the complementary colours gave us our brown.

3 Dry-brush the crumpled paper with a dusting of gold or contrasting paint to highlight the fine wrinkling. Buff paper when dry.

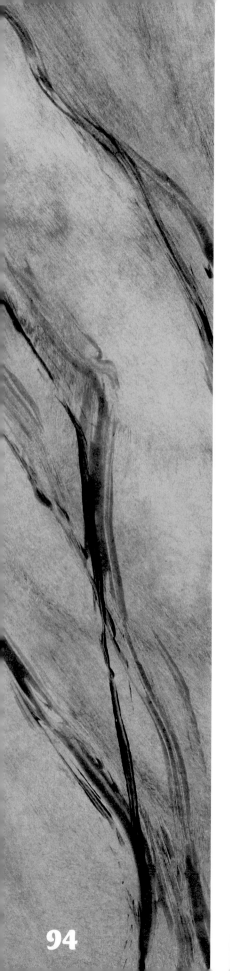

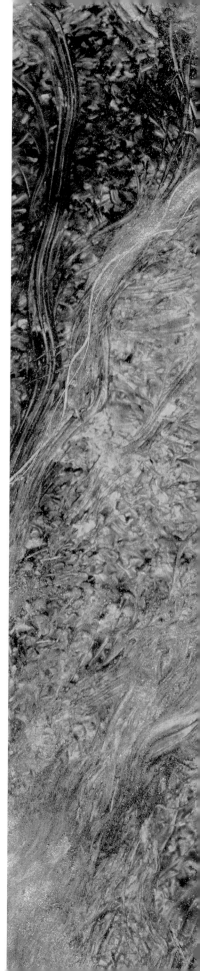

94

Veined marble

This faux marble effect can be used on its own or as a background for a rock theme.

1 Paint a pale wash across the paper. While wet, paint a slightly darker colour in diagonal wavy lines, joining them here and there. Repeat across the paper, leaving some background showing through. Soften by brushing over gently with a sponge or brush, first in the same direction as your lines, then in the opposite direction, slightly blurring them.

2 Repeat as many times as you wish, each time with a slightly darker or toning colour, filling in more of the background, though still leaving some of it showing.

3 Use a feather to drag the darkest colour over the paper, twirling it as you go. This will create very uneven, interesting veins. You can soften these too and repeat if necessary.

Malachite

Malachite is a green stone and traditionally this paint technique is done in green. Any range of harmonious colours works well, though, and we were happy to do our sample in brown, which looks a little like tree fungus. The hexagonal box lid on page 14 has been card-combed with blue-green fabric paint to simulate the rich tones of real malachite. It's a quick way of decorating large sheets of paper using transparent based paints or glazes.

1 Bend and tear a piece of stiff card into a rough edge.

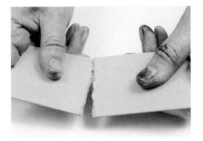

2 Paint PVA glaze onto paper and comb the rough-edged card in circular patterns all over the paper, resembling malachite.

As a variation, comb straight or criss-cross patterns.

Lapis lazuli

The rich, dark blue colours of the lapis lazuli precious stone with its striking veins are always attractive, but the faux effect can be achieved using any range of harmonious colours and sparkle dust or glitter.

1 Brush a layer of glaze or fabric paint extender onto paper.

2 Apply your chosen colour (dark blue if for traditional lapis lazuli) with a wall painting brush in any direction. Use a sea sponge or bubble wrap to create a texture on this layer of colour. Apply more paint with the sponge or bubble wrap to darken certain areas.

3 While the paint is still wet, twirl and drag a feather across the paper to resemble veins. Before the paint dries, tap a little gold powder here and there to add sparkle to your lapis effect.

Raised effects

Raised effects or relief may be achieved in many ways and usually, though not always, entails glue or heat somewhere along the line! The papers created with these techniques can be works of art in their own right, but will be equally striking used for cards or on gift boxes.

Top right: *A barefoot angel with attitude made from various handmade papers moulded with wall-paper paste around a salad-dressing bottle. The hair is glued together from torn shreds of brown and grey sisal paper decorated with fine fibres of gold lamé thread. The face, neck, torso and bare feet are moulded from small pieces of brown Mopane paper gently highlighted with bronze craft paint. The wrap-around dress of buff-coloured elephant-dung paper is highlighted with a light brushing of gold dust in matt varnish. The border detail on the dress hem is a strip of papyrus edged with liquid beads (fine seed beads in clear craft glue) applied with a palette knife. A piece of sticky-backed real copper tape used by stained glass artists forms the edging, and the shawl is a piece of coconut-matted fibre, straight from a palm on a Zanzibar beach.*

The wings are Japanese lace paper threaded with coir fibres, fastened with spotted guinea fowl feathers.

Opposite page: *It is always nice to receive a beautifully wrapped gift that shows care and thought. While it's easy enough to buy gift wrap these days, we've created our own special bags and boxes with not too much effort. The large gift bag at the back was made from vellum with detail added in silver with a leaf stencil. The silver-threaded cord handle just finished it off.*

The set of three gold decorated boxes was sprayed with gold paint. Stencils of lace, circle block outs and a waste strip left from sequin-making were used. Details were added with gold embossing powder.

A really simple way to wrap anything flat is to use a white paper bag – especially if you have quite a few similar ones to do. We added an orange stripe to ours, stamping off with a leaf stamp while the paint was wet. When the paint was dry we slipped in our gift, added some ribbon and raffia, a skeleton leaf and we were done.

The small black pyramid box was stamped with opaque and metallic paints using leaves as stamps.

The off-centre sparkly floral design on the black CD box is glue dots which were covered in foil, while the black and brown CD box was decorated by stamping bleach onto the box in a chess-board pattern to take the colour out. Leaf drawings were done in the gaps with a gold milky pen. Ribbon and raffia finished it all off.

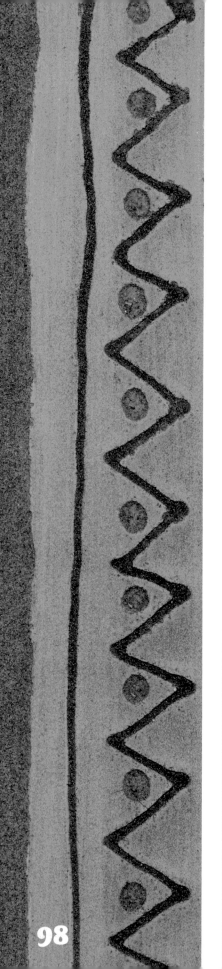

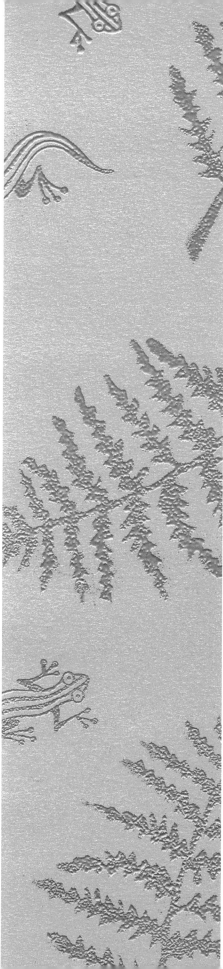

Sandy patterns

The simplest way of creating a raised effect is to add glue to an area and to attach whatever comes to hand! We used sand in different colours to make this pattern.

1 Add glue for one colour of sand at a time, otherwise the whole sheet will be covered at once. Use a nozzle for thin lines and a paintbrush for larger areas.

2 While still tacky, cover with sand and allow to dry.

3 Pour off excess sand to be used again and repeat for the next colour.

Other ideas for additions, apart from the normal ones like glitter and sequins and tiny beads, could be eggshells, fur and tea leaves. Rooibos tea leaves are a wonderful colour– we used them through a stencil for a quick-art block (see pages 104-105).

Embossed motifs

Stamps come in a wide range, from large-motif foam, through finer detailed rubber and metal stamps. Some suppliers turn your own designs into stamps for a very reasonable price (see dung-beetle stamp on page 134). The fern and lizard stamps in our sample were embossed with gold powder. Unless you are using clear embossing powder, which we did on some of our beads, it doesn't matter what colour ink is used to stamp.

1 Stamp your image in any colour ink in a pattern covering the page.

2 Cover the damp stamped lines with embossing powder. Tap the paper from behind the image or blow over the stamped area to loosen the excess powder onto a clean sheet of paper and funnel back into the container for re-use.

3 Heat with a heat gun or place under a grill until embossing powder melts.

Puff-paint motifs

Puff paint can be applied with a paintbrush or liner bottle. When dry, it is heated with a heat gun or even under a grill. The paint swells or puffs up (hence the name) leaving a much raised or 'popped corn' effect. Our rose-box examples on page 127 show this to great effect. We think we have created a rather classy effect with our 'ironed' stencil in this example where we have used gold coated paper.

1 Apply puff paint to paper in the window areas of a flower stencil. Dab off any excess paint. Allow to dry.

2 Place a piece of paper on top and then iron. The result is a slightly raised effect with a velvety feel similar to flocking with velvet or fabric jacquard.

3 Apply dots of paint between the stencilled flowers and heat without covering for the normal puffed up effect.

99

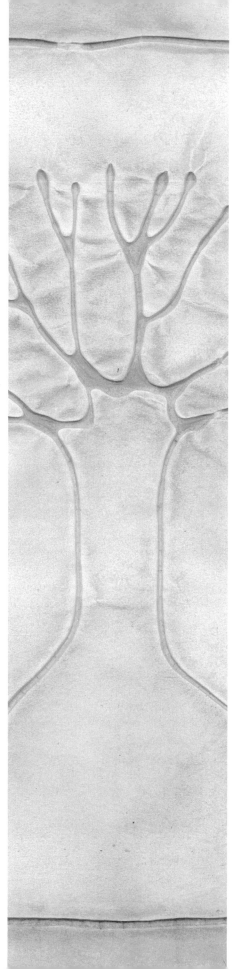

Talc embossing

Talcum powder makes a simple but softer variation of sand relief on paper. It is also a homemade substitute for flocking powder, though not as raised. While sand adds its own colour to paper, stamped images raised by talc must be dry brushed to show off their design. Long strips of paper stamped or stencilled in this way would make interesting wall-paper friezes or borders especially suited to Tuscan finishes.

1 Cover a simple stamp with wood glue and stamp randomly on your paper. While still tacky, cover with talcum powder and allow to dry. Shake off excess talc and blow the paper clean before proceeding.

2 Dry brush the page to show off the stamped motifs.

Flocking fibres add a velvety texture to glued designs on a surface, for example jacquard wall-papers.

Starch liner

Mix a thin paste of flour and water to the consistency of pancake mixture — it must be able to be squeezed through a nozzled bottle and keep its shape. Add a sprinkle of powdered cloves or wall-paper glue to the mixture to preserve it and keep the bugs away. Once the starch lines have been painted they are effectively sealed and hopefully no longer appeal to any hungry bug. If in doubt, however, seal with clear lacquer spray on the front and back of the paper.

1 Draw design lines with the starch paste on copy paper.

2 When dry, the raised lines will have buckled the paper slightly but this adds to the effect. Flatten under a pile of books.

3 Dry-brush paint over the raised lines to colour them, and fill in the background.

Starch reverse variation

We dry brushed the geometric African design as a reverse of the starch outline technique. In other words, we were not dry brushing the starch lines themselves but rather highlighting the embossed effect they leave on the back of the paper with the dry brush colour. The heavily textured and slightly buckled paper in a looping design was used for one of the quick art blocks on page 104.

1 Squeeze starch lines on one side of your paper. Allow to dry thoroughly. Turn the paper over and dry brush the reverse side of the paper catching colour up against the embossed lines.

2 We painted within these lines with more solid colour to emphasize areas of the pattern.

Embossed rubbing

Creating a raised or embossed effect is also possible without heat or glue. Use a stencil and an embossing tool, or the eraser at the end of a pencil, which also works well. If you need to see your stencil more clearly through the paper for positioning, use a light box or lift the paper up to the window. This technique is perfect for card making or adding lettering or motif detail to scrapbooking pages.

1 Place the paper over the stencil and rub gently into the grooves with your chosen implement. Make as many impressions as you want. Your paper can be used this way up or turned over for a raised effect.

2 Dry brush colour over the paper to allow the relief to stand out more.

White on white is subtle and classy. For a more raised embossing, work on a padded surface.

Wax rubbing

Brass rubbing of engravings is a popular pastime. Make your own brass rubbing on plain paper for a special effect or repeat the design across a large piece of paper for interesting gift wrap. A child can do this technique quickly and easily using coins. Small, detailed stencils also work well.

1 Lay a flat cut-out shape (from card, plastic or metal film) onto a surface. We used a flat brass decoration.

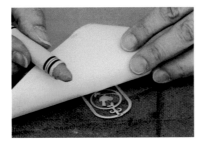

2 Place a clean sheet of paper over the shape. Rub over the area with the side of a wax crayon. The image will show up as though it is in relief. Cover the page randomly with rubbings in several shades of the same colour or in harmonious colours to create quick wrapping paper.

Secure the rubbing shape with double-sided tape to prevent shifting while rubbing.

Texture paste

This will shrink somewhat when dry but it stays very flexible because the paste is applied in a thin layer. You can also colour the texture paste with some paint before applying it. This could be used in any number of ways for a quick art project.

1 Apply textured paste all over the paper with a palette knife or strip of flexible plastic cut from a credit card.

2 Allow to dry and paint or dry brush over dried paste.

Add further raised effects with a stencil, as in the paste section to follow, or add interesting bits and pieces such as sequins – texture paste holds small embedded items quite successfully.

Paste

Whole books have been written on paste papers so we had to include some examples here! The idea is to coat the paper with coloured paste and then create various effects. The paste keeps for quite a long time in the fridge – if it thickens too much, just add water and whisk. Add colour with inks, paints or pigments. While this takes at least a day to dry, it does not make the paper buckle and has a soft leathery feel. If the thought of actually cooking any-thing makes you weak – fabric paint works really well in a similar way, though it's not quite as textured. Adding colour to wall-paper paste would also work.

Paste papers are usually used in bookbinding, but we have used them on some of the quick art blocks for a simple, slightly three-dimensional effect. In all our examples we have kept the paste relatively thick, but it may be watered down for a thinner finish. There is no need to apply any kind of fixative, though spraying with clear lacquer spray will strengthen the paper.

Our paste recipe: cook 1 part flour, 1 part sugar and 2 parts water to a thick roux. Add a sprinkling of ground cloves as a preservative (yum!). Mix thoroughly and add your colour. The more you add, the darker the result.

Right: A quick-art project using subtly coloured decorated paper glued onto supawood boxes to show them off. We used various textured papers, many of them off-cuts and left-overs, to add extra dimension, using very simple techniques found throughout the book. The top box in the niche was mosaic-board stamped with a spiral onto silk paper. The centre box paper came from our crack-filler sample. For the third box lines of paste were drawn onto sisal paper with a liner bottle and detail was added in gold. The top box of the collection in the arch was made from Japanese lace-paper stuck onto a coffee tinted square. The dried tea bags (remove tea leaves!) in the next box add a quirky touch and tickled our Rooibos-loving publisher no end! Detail was added with gold leaf. The labyrinth was scraped into monoprinted paste paper and shadows added with a brush. The box below teabags was covered in embossed handmade paper and lightly shaded with fabric paint to show off a three-dimensional circle within a square. To the right of this, a mesh printed "accident" was detailed with a stencil of glued Rooibos tea leaves. The gold paper box, far left on the bottom row, had paste applied and a pattern scraped onto it. Papyrus covered the next box and what more fitting stamp than an the eye of Horus, the Egyptian symbol for good health? A looping pattern of reverse starch embossing was dry brushed and stuck on the second last box. The darker paper on the final box was left over from mesh printing, while the lighter piece was cut from a happy accident! We could have carried on and on as this was great fun.

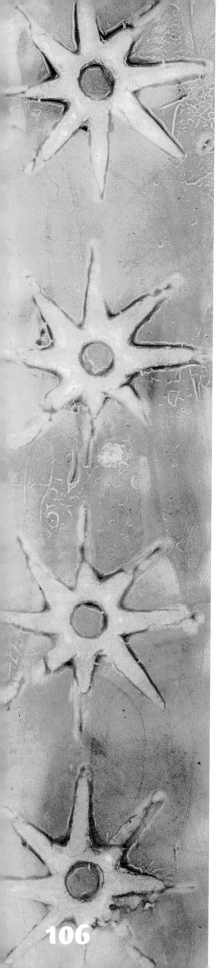

Impressed motifs

Stamps are always a good option when wanting to repeat a motif and this is no exception. The stamps we used in this example are Ghanaian Adinkra stamps and part of Angie's prized collection. The one she is using is a symbol of courage and defiance. The stamped impression in the background is the chief Adinkra motif and forms the basis of Adinkra printing.

1 Apply paste to the entire piece of paper as evenly as possible, using a credit card or spatula.

2 Push a simple stamp into the paste to create an impressed image. Repeat as necessary.

3 Leave to dry. The thickness and evenness of the paste will determine how much of a raised effect will be obtained.

Layered paste

For this technique, coloured paste is applied to the entire paper, with a second, darker coloured layer applied in the form of a stencilled design. While we have used a palette knife to apply the initial paste layer and left it to dry, one could scrape into this as in the next technique and then add a stencil to that. There is also no reason to use only one colour. A number of harmonious colours could also be applied, so that they merge into one another, creating a more colourful finish.

1 Apply the paste to the paper with a palette knife or credit card or other implement as roughly as you like, creating a very textured effect. Allow to dry.

2 Place a stencil in position on the paper and apply paste.

3 Lift the stencil gently to reveal the raised motif and allow to dry thoroughly.

Scraped patterns

This is the most common technique used in paste-paper designs. Although we used a special scraping tool (available from most hardware stores), you can use just about any implement for scraping, depending on the effect you wish to achieve. A fork will give thin lines, a rubber eraser thicker lines, any of which can be repeated at will. Here again, we have used only one colour, but a combination of harmonious colours will work just as well. See our examples of the squiggly lines and labyrinth on our quick-art blocks on the previous page. While we used fabric paint for our beach bags, this technique would have worked equally well with a thin paste.

1 Apply paste to the entire piece of paper, as evenly as possible.

2 Use a scraper, fork or other implement to scrape across the paper leaving wavy or straight lines, or creating a weave pattern as we did here.

Marbling

Marbling is a decorative technique which results in fine-grained swirls and spotty patterns similar to those found in many different types of marble, granite and other precious stones, and is how the process came to be named. It is not limited to any colour range and can be deliberately manipulated into myriads of patterns depending on the carrier used to float inks or paints. The techniques covered in this section use water, shaving cream and extender as carriers for the paint, which allow random mixing and patterns to be formed. You never know what the outcome is going to be, which adds to the fun.

Top right: A good example of just how versatile paper beads can be, this chandelier has around 1 000 beads! To make the beads, about 80 pieces of A4 paper were painted with fabric paint in magenta, red and a little bright orange for sparkle. While wet, the paper was scraped using forks and other scrapers to add texture and interest. The beads were made like those used for the jewellery (see pages 78-79), and ordinary beads threaded with them to add to the effect.

Right: The beads for this key holder or bag tassel by Heather were made with one piece of marbled paper chosen for its colour. The widths of the triangles varied greatly so the beads were all different lengths. We covered the large bead with paper too and embossed the lot with sparkle powder.

Bottom right: The large sheet of paper for this scrapbook album-cover was painted with a big wall brush in quick strokes of fiery red, yellow and orange and varnished for strength. The album lettering was a lot more finicky – each letter cut three times in graduated sizes from different patterned papers and layered. The top letters were decorated with variegated metal leaf skewings. For the scrapbook pages we gave scrapbooking friends sets of decorated paper and photographs which they used in pleasing combinations.

Opposite page: The kite was made from drinking straws, threaded with string to make individual tetrahedrons tied together after covering with paper on two sides – one A3 covered one tetrahedron. The three central papers were painted with red, orange and yellow fabric paint using rough brushstrokes, and scrunched off while the paint was still wet. The rest of the papers were variations on a theme with various resists placed on wet paper. Watered down acrylic paint in shades of yellow and orange was dropped on, allowing them to run into each other while drying. This textured paper would also be successful for scrapbooking pages.

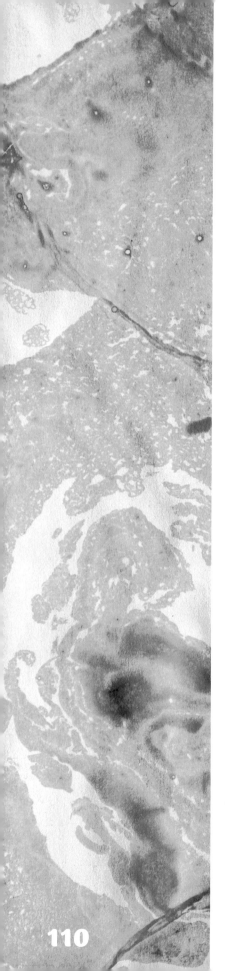
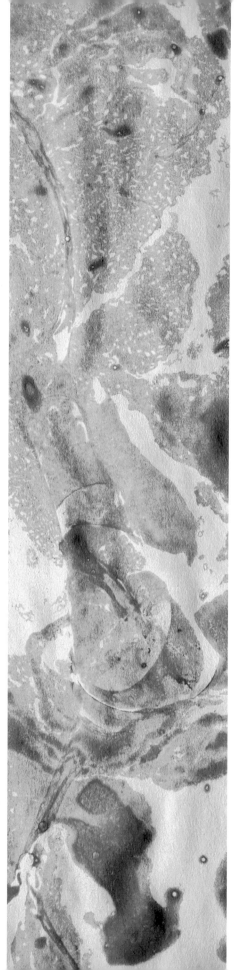

Oil-paint marbling

This is the simplest and easiest way to achieve a marble effect on paper – although the fumes can be quite off-putting. We found it a pretty hit and miss affair but great fun and the unpredictable results were wonderful in themselves. The whole process became quite addictive and if we'd been working indoors we'd probably have become high on turpentine! The finished papers take a few days to dry properly and will still have a slightly waxy, oily feel; so if they are to be written on it is best to iron them first between two clean sheets of absorbent paper to seal them. We have used black and white marbled papers for the blotter, writing paper, pen holder and photo frame on pages 138-139.

1 Dilute chosen oil colours with white spirits or mineral turpentine until they are quite runny – the consistency of thin cream, as all the experts say!

2 Drop these thinned oil colours onto water in a roasting pan. The temperature of the water and various other factors can affect the way the oils spread over the water surface. This is where the hit and miss bit comes in. In serious traditional marbling you would use a floater solution or thickener for your water and float the oil drops at certain intervals and manipulate them into incredible patterns. We decided to dispense with all this as our method is more fun and less head-ache producing! After you have dropped your oils and hopefully they have spread over the surface and not dive-bombed to the bottom of the pan (if they do just add more turps and try again), swirl through the colours gently with a comb, toothpick or needle.

3 Hold a sheet of paper at opposite corners and roll it quickly onto the water surface. Allow the paper to settle briefly and lift it off by grasping it on opposite sides and letting the water drip back into the pan as you raise the paper.

4 Place the marbled paper flat on a sheet of glass or plastic and pour a cup of water over it to wash off the excess oil paint. Allow to dry flat.

5 Clean the water surface by skimming it with torn newspaper strips before marbling your next piece, or marble more paper, creating lighter and more subtle effects until the water is clear.

Acrylic paint

Acrylic paints or inks need a floater for marbling and while there are specialized floaters available we used wall-paper paste, mixed according to the instructions, and then added the same amount of water again. As this is usually paler and not oil based, it makes excellent writing paper.

1 Pour the floater into a container big enough to lay a piece of paper. If using thick acrylic paint, this will have to be thinned with water to a runny consistency. Flick or drop this onto the floater.

2 Use a fork to drag a pattern through the ink and floater.

3 When you are satisfied with the pattern, lay the paper gently on top and tap it to remove all air bubbles.

4 Remove the paper and lay flat where the excess floater can be removed with soft paper or cloth.

111

Nail-varnish marbling

This is a creative way of using up discarded nail varnishes. Marbled onto glossy photo paper they produce an exotic, encrusted paper. You can use solvent-based glass paint as well.

1 Dilute varnishes with acetone, working in a well ventilated area. Acetone is highly flammable so don't allow any flames while you are using it.

2 Drop small amounts of thinned varnish onto water in a roasting pan. The varnish will quickly spread across the pan and become increasingly 'crinkled' as more drops are added.

3 Quickly roll a sheet of photo paper glossy side down onto the water surface as for oil marbling and lift it in the same way. Turn over and let the paper lie flat until dry. Re-marble if patchy for extra depth and an encrusted texture.

Shaving cream

A fun alternative to conventional marbling, this is addictive! We used ink but watered-down paint will do. Patterns are more easily controlled and manipulated with this method.

1 Spread good quality shaving cream evenly over a piece of plastic larger than your paper. Drop ink or liquid paint onto the shaving cream.

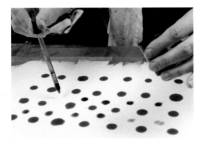

2 Use a fork or other implement to drag a pattern through the colour in waves, straight lines or spirals.

3 Lay the paper on top and gently run your finger over the back to make sure all the air bubbles are removed.

4 Lift the paper, place on a piece of waste paper and scrape off the excess shaving cream.

The shaving cream may be used over and over but each subsequent print will become more blurred.

Fabric-paint marbling

The steps are very similar to those used for marbling with shaving cream. In the absence of a carrier or floater, a more solid effect is achieved. In our example coloured paper was used as a base, which in itself changes the ultimate effect.

1 Coat a piece of plastic larger than your paper with a layer of fabric paint, using a credit card. Drop small blobs of two harmonious colours onto this.

2 Scrape a pattern into the paint with a skewer, fork or other implement to create a design.

3 Lay the paper on top and gently run your finger over the back to remove any air bubbles. Lift and place on a piece of waste paper and remove the excess fabric paint by scraping with a credit card.

Spray painting

As with so many other techniques, there are a number of ways to spray paint, but liquid paint or ink is always used. The most professional way to spray is to use a spray gun for large pieces or an artist's airbrush for finer work. An easy way out, although a bit expensive and with less control, is to use a spray can. Artists' atomizers, sometimes called diffusers, are also a cheaper option than an airbrush – and are good for your lungs! Smokers beware – you may hyperventilate trying to puff through these! The easiest and most affordable options, are toothbrushes and spray bottles, though the effect is not as even. While the stunning orange pockets on these photographs were not spray painted, they introduce this vibrant colour which we chose for our spray-painted examples.

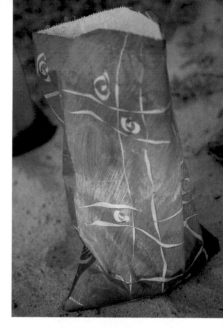

Opposite page and right: What amazing ambiance these bags created at dawn on the beach at Kreeftebaai! The idea of placing bags filled with sand and a lit candle down a drive for a special occasion is not new, but we always feel that a little colour wouldn't go amiss, so we painted a wad of white bags on both sides (wait for one side to dry before painting the other) using fabric paint in different orange tones. We scraped various patterns into the wet paint using rubber scrapers. Fabric paint dries to a slightly plastic finish on paper which strengthens the bag. The paste technique would also work for a project like this. Put extra cloves in the mixture, and you have a fragrant bonus!

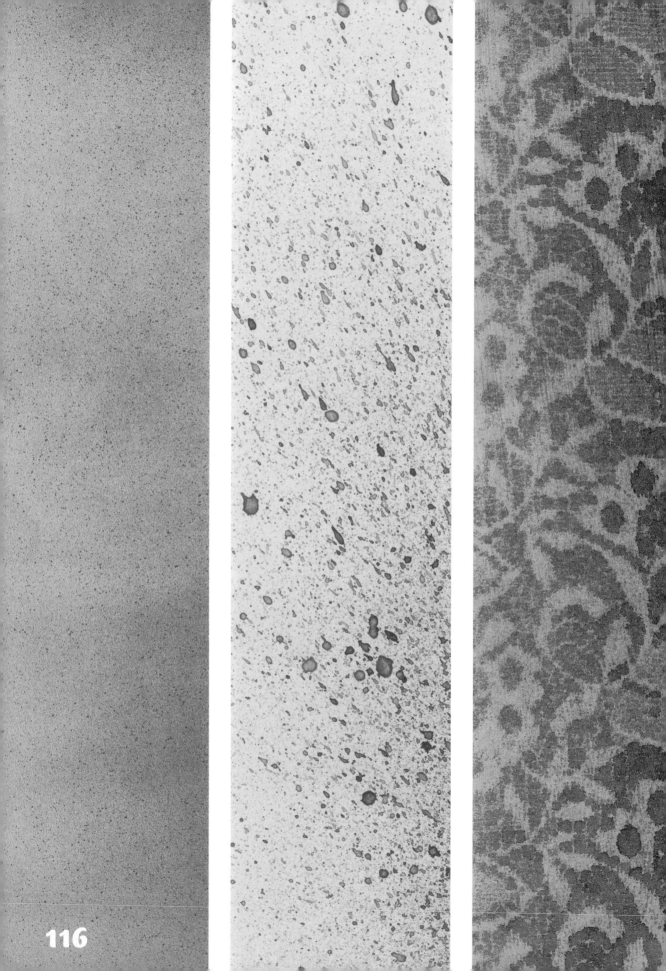

Spray cans

Spray paint dries almost instantly and is the beloved medium of graffiti artists. Used on paper, it gives a soft, slightly cloudy effect. Always follow the manufacturer's instructions when using spray paint. As the fumes are very we suggest you work outside, or in a very well ventilated area. We used neon paint, hence the strong colour.

1 Secure paper to a firm support and hold vertically.

2 Follow instructions on the can and hold it upright while spraying from the recommended distance.

It's that simple! This is great for stencils but does not work well as a background unless you will be using oil paints over it.

Spattered paint

This effect resembles the speckles or freckles on a hen's egg! Directing the paint may be a bit tricky, so do a few practice runs to perfect the technique. Experiment with different paint and toothbrushes. . This technique was used to add texture spots in the faux granite technique but can be used on its own to produce very interesting papers using a minimum of paint. Dilute left-over bits of paint by adding a little warm water to their containers and shaking well to dissolve the colours before dipping your brush directly into them. Protect your clothing whn you do this!

1 Dip a toothbrush or small, stiff bristled brush into paint and pull your fingers over the bristles, releasing a fine spatter of paint.

2 Repeat the process in varying colours for a more interesting speckled effect.

Sprayed patterns

Lace patterns are a pretty and easy option to use on their own or as an addition to an already decorated piece of paper. We used lace on one of the gift boxes on page 97 and sprayed it with gold spray paint. Set the spray nozzle on the bottle for a fine misty spray and practise first to get the ink going.

1 It is best to be able to angle the paper in some way, perhaps on a board. Place the lace onto the paper, making sure it can't slip off.

2 Spray evenly across the lace. Do not overspray as the lace will become wet and smudge the paint.

3 Lay the paper down gently and remove the lace to reveal a reverse image of the lace pattern.

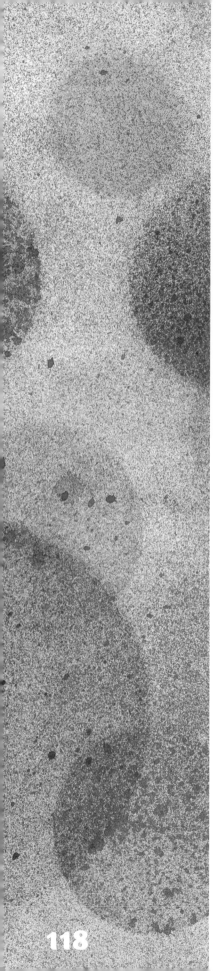

Atomizer stencils

Using an atomizer with stencils adds a quite different effect and is really quick to do as the paint dries fast. Large pieces of paper are quite manageable, as long as you have the breath! Atomizing diffusers can be bought at art shops. The trick is to hold the two metal tubes at their most extended angle, to insert the thin tube in the liquid paint, to take a deep breath (from your stomach!) and to blow slowly and evenly though the wider tube. The paint will spray out in a fine mist. Direct this at the paper. Do a few practice runs on scrap paper first.

1 Spray the paper evenly with the lightest colour and allow to dry. Use coloured paper if you do not want a fine speckled background.

2 Place the stencil in position and blow a fine spray through the metal diffuser. Take care not to overspray as the paint will run.

3 Remove the stencil and repeat as many times and in as many colours as you wish.

Masked patterns

Just about anything can be used as a mask or a positive stencil (also see stencilling on pages 44-49). For this example we used willow leaves on soft peach-coloured paper. This versatile paper could be used for scrapbooking projects, cards, as gift wrap and done in softer colours as a background for other techniques. You can use any spray-paint tool.

1 Place the leaves on the paper and spray evenly over them with your chosen spray tool.

2 Leave these leaves in position and add more. Spray again, either the same colour or one slightly different.

3 Wait for the ink to dry and carefully lift off the leaves.

Monoprinting

Monoprinting is generally done with rigid plastic (PVC or bleached X-rays), glass (take care to bevel the edges) or even your work table surface. The idea is to paint your image onto one surface and then to transfer it onto paper. This makes a print which is the reverse of the original. Monoprinting is best suited to bold designs, done quite quickly, before the paint dries. In this section we have included some other ways of monoprinting for variation.

Top right: *While these cards were all made with off-cuts and left-over decorated paper, all the decorating ideas in this book are ideal for unique and special cards. For the fishy card Debbie tore a wax negative from the piece of paper used to protect the iron from the batik sample on page 60. She also made the red and yellow collage card from scraps of red painted spun bond and oil marbling glued onto more spun bond and white card. For the woven card, slits were cut into the front and thin off-cuts woven into them – a great way to use up slivers of decorated paper. Sarie very cleverly cut the rhino from a stencil laid onto some marbled paper – she even positioned a spot for the eye! This was glued to some granite paper and framed simply with white card on black.*

Bottom right: *The greenish square card was made from the off cuts of a piece of stamped gift wrap with small nuts and washers glued in the middle. On the next card, wisps of red spun bond create an abstract on a leaf printed piece left over from some gold and autumn shaded wrapping paper. This was framed with a brown dragged card glued to a white backing. In similar vein strips of varying widths of the wrapping paper and the red spun bond were arranged simply on a piece of gold dragged paper (bottom left). The final card on our string was made to show off a weathered oyster shell. Sarie glued finely corrugated lilac paper, gold, purple Canson, wood-grained and yellow colour-washed paper rectangles in layers to form an interesting frame.*

Opposite page: *Once you realize how easy it is to make your own gift wrap, you'll never buy any again. The basic method for most of this gift wrap was the same: various fabric paint colours were painted roughly with a wall brush onto large sheets of paper making sure that it was well covered. It was either left to dry as is (red roll second from right), or motifs scraped into the paint (red roll far right). The brown roll in the centre was textured by dabbing with scrunched up paper, with metallic dust adding some sparkle. The colourful roll on the left (bottom) was covered in cling film and left to dry. The centre roll in magenta and orange was a complete accident. While mixing the colours I cleaned off a tongue depressor I was using on a clean piece of paper and I liked the pattern I was making, so I carried on. Most of the techniques discussed in the book are suitable for creating gift wrap in no time.*

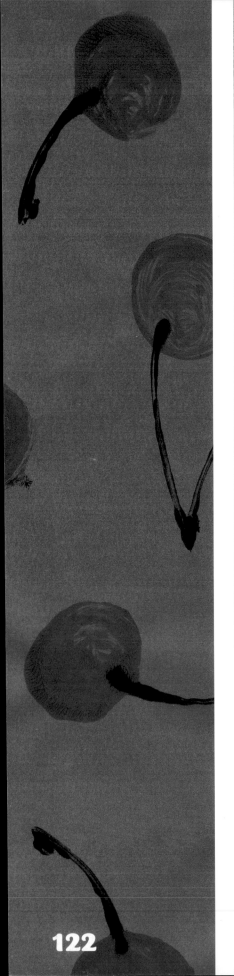

Monoprinted motifs

We used a simple cherry design, painted and printed in one go. More complex images can be built up in layers, using the first print as a guide. This is a great technique for special cards, scrapbooking pages or smaller sheets of gift wrap. It is a particularly good technique to include in collage work. We printed on red card stock

1 Paint a circle in red paint (fabric paint, craft paint or acrylic) onto a piece of rigid plastic. Paint a slightly curved line from just inside the circle outwards in green. This transparent green dried brown on the red paper we used, but would appear green if printed on white paper.

2 Place the plastic paint-side down on your paper and rub over gently to make your print. We painted and printed the cherries one or two at a time, so that the paint did not dry before printing – very important with acrylics as they dry fast.

Sandwich print

This technique is great for creating texture for its own sake, or for overprinting on decorated paper. We printed in red on red. While we used small glass and plastic squares for the sample, this could be done on a larger scale. We did this with paste and paper for our quick art project (see page 104) creating a lovely rippled texture in which we scraped a labyrinth.

1 Apply paint to a piece of glass or plastic and cover with another piece of glass or plastic. Different plastics will give slightly different textures, as will glass.

2 Pull the sandwich apart and use the two halves to print. Repeat as many times as needed.

Two pieces of glass together are harder to pull apart than plastic, so take care not to smudge your texture pattern before printing.

Patterned prints

This, too, can be used on already decorated or patterned paper to enhance the pattern, or for its own charm. We printed in red on red again. The darker yellow paper on the bottom outer sections of the kite on page 109 was decorated with this technique.

1 Apply a thin, even layer of paint to a sheet of plastic.

2 Draw into it with a skewer, back of a brush or even your finger or whatever else comes to hand.

3 When you are satisfied with the pattern, place the plastic paint-side down onto your paper and rub with your hand to make an even print.

4 Lift off the plastic to reveal your pattern.

Don't worry if you make mistakes; you can always rub out your pattern and start again before you print.

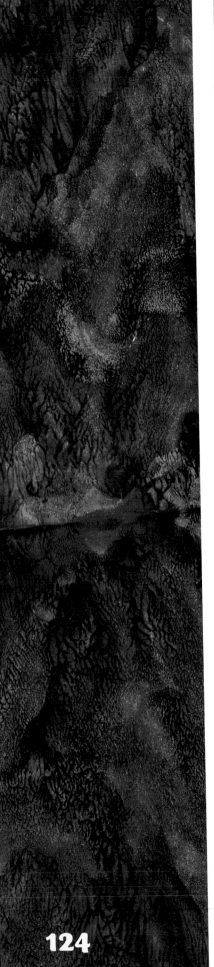
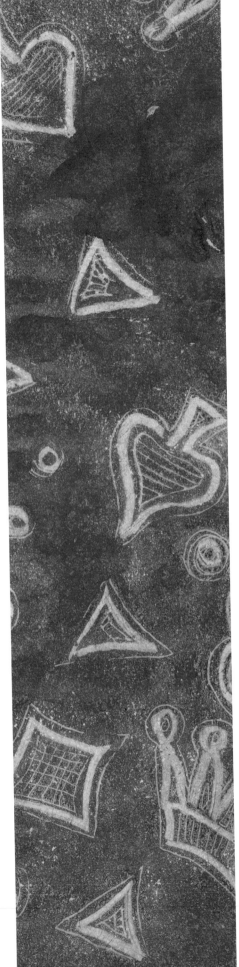
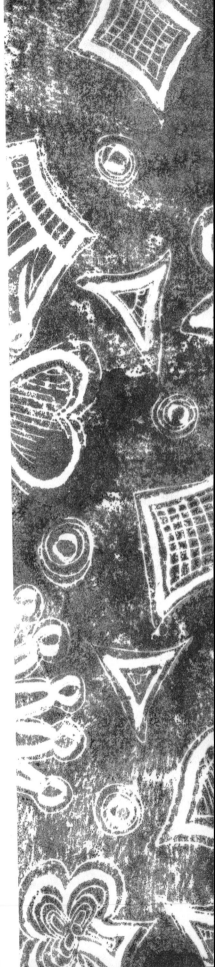

Mirror-image printing

These mirror-image monoprints are done by sandwiching paint between folds of paper like we all did in pre-school. Every time we do one it's completely different from the previous one! Crop these pieces asymmetrically to make interesting cards.

1 Fold paper in half, crease and then open out flat again.

2 On one side of the fold paint thick blobs of chosen colours onto the paper.

3 Close the fold over the paint blobs and smooth the paper down.

4 Open the fold carefully – the paint will pull apart in a feathery-textured, mirror image smudged design. Play with patterns or design leaves and butterflies – or go abstract and bold as we did.

Ironed wax-transfer

This is a very simple form of monoprinting or wax-transfer printing. You can use either wax crayons or oil pastels. It's a good technique to do with children although adult supervision and assistance will be necessary for the ironing process.

1 Draw line designs you wish to transfer on a piece of paper, or coat one piece of paper with thick wax or oil pastels for a scraped design.

2 Scrape patterns into the coating with toothpicks, skewers or even your fingernails, all of which will give you different line widths.

3 Place the design down onto a clean sheet of paper.

4 Iron carefully by lifting and replacing the iron in different areas covering the paper.

5 If you slide the iron over the paper, the hot wax or oil smudges easily and the scraped pattern in particular will simply melt into a solid mass of colour. This could be very disappointing after all your efforts, so take great care when you apply the heat!

6 For a complete transfer, draw or rub oil pastels (not wax crayons) onto baking parchment; reverse lettering if using. Iron parchment face down onto copy paper. The oil pastels will be almost completely transferred onto the copy paper, leaving the baking parchment clean enough for re-use.

Bits & snips

There are some paper-decorating techniques that are just not as easy to fit into categories as others. Vegetable dyeing has loads of possibilities, but we chose beetroot as it really suited the colouring for this section. Transfers can involve several techniques and have many applications. On the following pages we discuss a number of unusual options.

Opposite page and right: If pink is your colour, this one's for you. A beautifully decorated box filled with goodies for batht-time bliss becomes part of a treasured gift (enjoy, Rowina!). The paper for the lid of the smaller box and the body of the large box was painted with acrylic paint, covered with cling film and left to dry. A darker pink was brushed over some of this paper to create a slightly different texture for the woven strips of the small box. Strips of paper for the weave pattern were glued to the bottom of the box and folded over the rim before being glued neatly to the inside. This was done over the lighter textured paper. Once both boxes were covered with the textured paper, the roses and leaves were painted with a brush in puff paint, as well as the stripes along the sides of the bigger lid, with dots between the stripes and along the lower rim of the box. The puff paint was heated in the conventional way with a heat gun or hair dryer so that it puffed up. Thin silver lines were added to the stripes with milky pen and silver dots on the weave pattern completed the picture. Take care to work really neatly when covering boxes — rough corners and slack folds will detract from your creativity and effort to produce a unique presentation box.

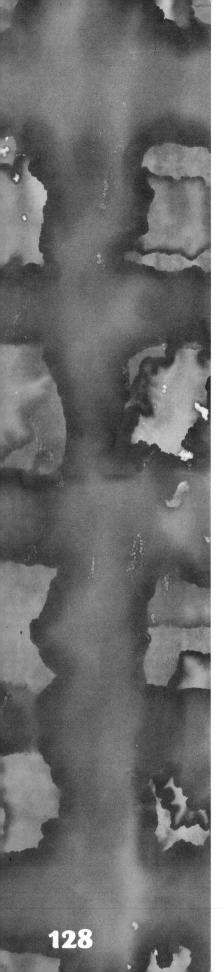

Vegetable dyeing

Vegetables can be cut and printed onto paper for interesting effects. Cut onions leave concentric patterns and their boiled skins boiled make a wonderful dye and handmade paper. Beetroot must be the easiest and most dramatic veggie to transfer colour to paper. You have to cook them for the best effect, but we have a short cut!

1 Place a few scrubbed beetroot in a glass-covered casserole dish in enough water to cover and microwave about 30 minutes on high.

2 Pour off beetroot juice and paint it onto paper. Allow to dry. The paper will have a softer, thicker, more flexible feel when dry.

3 Paint over with water to create interesting blotting patterns or try spraying water drops and watch a spotty pattern appear.

Thinners transfer

Lacquer thinners or acetone works well for transferring sections of images. Work in a well-ventilated area when doing this, as thinners fumes are toxic. It is also not advisable for children to do this without adult supervision — if at all. Ordinary black and white photocopied designs may be transferred or, as we have done here, use sections of pictures from magazines to build up a new image. It is best to keep your design or picture simple. This creates an ethereal, fantasy feel.

1 Tear interesting pictures out of magazines for their colours. The less glossy ones work best — very glossy pages don't work at all.

2 Draw the basic outlines of your intended picture, on a suitable background paper, to help you position the transfers. Cut out the reverse of the shapes that you want to fill with transferred colour from the torn magazine pages.

3 Place the cut-out face down in position on the paper. Soak a cotton wool ball in thinners and rub firmly over the back of the cut-out. Take care not to shift it while transferring the ink from the cutout to the drawn picture.

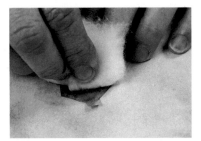

4 For a clearer image, you may need to burnish or rub the print with the back of a spoon or other smooth object.

5 Remove the cut-out, taking care not to smudge the transferred colour.

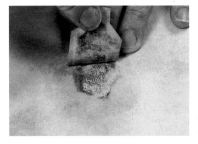

6 Continue adding prints in different areas, until your picture is built up.

7 Add definition to the shapes with pencil crayons for a subtle effect or pens or kokis for something more striking.

This is a good technique to use for unique greeting and birthday cards.

Lotion transfer

Inkjet-printed images can also be transferred by means of any water-based body lotion, hand cream or fabric paint extender – the water dissolves the inks used for inkjet printers. I experimented with this after one of my daughters' friends mentioned that she had used body lotion to transfer a newspaper print to a T-shirt.

1 Print your image using the flip function, especially if it has lettering.

2 Paint or sponge a thin layer of aqueous cream or extender carefully onto the front of the print. The inks may start to bleed so try not to rub too much. Place the print face down onto plain paper or card and smooth it down gently. It may stretch and bubble at this stage so work quickly and carefully.

3 Drop more cream or extender onto the back of the print and gently rub it all over with your fingertips until the cream has soaked into the paper, making the image visible from the wrong side.

4 Lift a corner of the print to check if it is transferring. Replace and rub (burnish) carefully with the back of a teaspoon all over for the clearest

transfer. Carefully peal off the print. Allow the transferred image to dry thoroughly.

Different types of paper give different effects. The clearest print resulted from copy paper to copy paper. Copy paper to card resulted in a slightly blurred image. The hot-pressed surface of the card to which this magenta photo collage sample was transferred didn't absorb the ink immediately; it smudged, causing a very interesting, almost wax-like texture – this inspired the background paper used in the next project: the paper sample shows both the inkjet image and its corresponding transfer in mirror image.

Transparent decals

Clear contact plastic, clear packaging tape, and ordinary shiny and matt sticky tape can be used to turn photocopies and prints into custom-made transparent decals or stickers – another form of transfer. Create your own decals from photographs using this method and superimpose them on special scrapbooking pages.

1 Cover the photocopies (face up) with pieces of clear contact or strips of packaging tape and sticky tape, depending on the size of transparent

decal or sticker required. Burnish (rub) the covered images with the back of a spoon or bone folder to eliminate any air bubbles between the tape and the print.

2 Cut the pieces of contact or strips of taped photocopies into the required sizes or shapes of transfer. Soak these in warm water for about 5 minutes.

3 Remove and gently rub the paper off the back of the pieces until only the printing ink remains on the clear contact or tape. The decals/transfers are now transparent and a little sticky, therefore repositionable. They can be re-shaped if desired and glued into place on paper with an ordinary glue stick if a stronger, more permanent bond is required.

This method only works well with photocopies on coated paper and magazine prints where the printed image is on the surface of the paper and not absorbed into the fibres of the paper.

Metallic effects

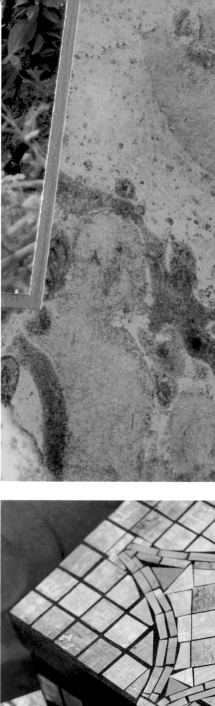

Shiny paints and other metallic bits add an irresistible lure to paper pages and projects. We have used them so far to add highlights here and there but felt the urge to include some really glitzy examples which demonstrate just some of the range of shines available, from glitters and sparkle dust to gold leaf. These effects can also be achieved with paints, most of which are available in water-based, oil and solvent varieties, so take your pick. We've tried to cover the range as concisely as possible — otherwise we'd have had to write another book. So raid your local hardware store, kitchen drawer and scrapbook nook and add some bling when you do your thing on paper!

Top right: The paper for this scrapbooking page was torn from a sheet of Ingres paper marbled with oil colours in lamp black, titanium white and viridian.

Bottom right: Who would have thought that a spiral staircase would be the inspiration for a simple diamond mosaic on a box? This is quite an interesting design progression and one that can be used in many different ways. The brown paper on these boxes was painted with fabric paint, textured with scrunched paper and sprinkled here and there with gold dust. The diamond pattern is a colour print of the pattern created in Microsoft Paint (see page 142-143). This was originally a photo of a spiral staircase which was flipped horizontally. These two images were joined and then flipped vertically which created the diamond shape with darker detail as seen on the small box. The medium sized box was covered with paper printed with an enlarged centre section of the diamond shape, with none of the dark visible. The mosaic was then worked out simplifying the diamond shape still further.

Opposite page: I decorated a large piece of thin card for these baskets, painting it on one side with red and green fabric paint (these complementaries make brown). When this was dry, I drew a pattern all over it in gold pastel crayons. As the pastels smudge, I sprayed the painted card with clear lacquer spray. The other side of the card (yes, you have to paint both sides!) was dragged with a very dark green — almost black — allowed to dry, and dry brushed with gold craft paint. To make the baskets I cut this card into strips of different widths for each basket (from 15 mm to 0,7 mm). All the baskets were woven from a square and then turned on the bias to weave the sides. They were finished off in different ways to create different styles. The star-shaped and small baskets had thin wire inserted into their rims so that they would hold their shape, while the front basket holds its shape owing to the weaving pattern.

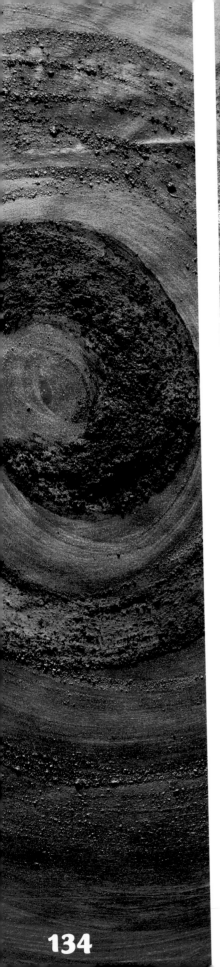

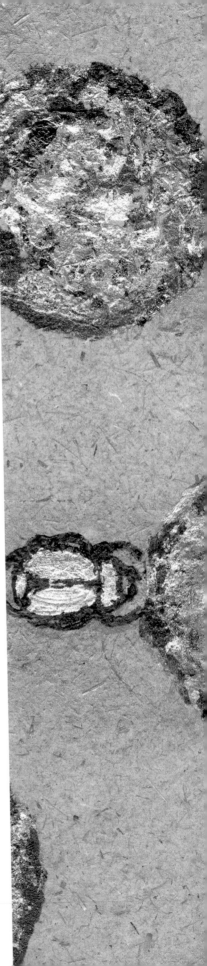

Rusty paper

Rust paint is available in many forms, from spray cans to a three-part process of undercoat, rust coat and rusting agents which produce different tones of rust, from red and brown through to yellow. We used the three-part process and added a sprinkling of filings to increase the depth of rust effect in the centre of the spiral.

1 Paint a large spiral in copper. We used conventional water-based craft paint for a shiny contrast to the rust effect. Allow to dry.

2 Paint a spiral of rust undercoat between the lines of the copper spiral. While this is still damp, overcoat with rust paint, dry and then paint on a second coat of rust paint. Sprinkle iron filing dust in the centre of the still wet rust paint.

3 Apply different coloured rust activators with a dropper and allow the effect to develop.

Gilded dung paper

Not all that glitters is gold – to a dung beetle a lovely pile of elephant dung is gold! The Egyptians elevated and gilded the dung beetle, or scarab, as a sacred amulet – a symbol of creation – and in particular its ball of dung as a golden sun being rolled across the sky. This was the inspiration for the gilding on this piece. We used sheets of gold and variegated metal leaf as well as gold, copper and bronze paint, gold powder and gold and bronze embossing powder.

1 Dry brush paper with gold craft paint.

2 Create dung-ball pathways by dry brushing copper and bronze craft paint in curved lines on the paper.

3 Use a jam jar lid to stamp rough circles of fabric paint extender here and there on the pathways for the dung balls. Cover patchily with bronze and gold embossing powder, shake off excess and heat with a heat gun or under a grill until the powder melts.

4 Dot the dung balls with more extender and dust with gilding powder to highlight. Dry with a hairdryer.

5 Dab tacky glue or gilding milk in patches all over the dung balls in the gaps between embossing. Allow to dry until tacky and gently place variegated metal leaf skewings (or bits) onto the glued patches. Rub with a brush until all loose leaf-bits are brushed off – save these for your skewings collection.

6 Stamp dung beetles in position at the dung balls and emboss with dark bronze embossing powder.

7 Paint tacky glue carefully on their backs and gild with gold leaf in the same way as the dung balls.

We used elephant-dung paper, but any textured, hand-made paper will do for this technique. If you cannot find a dung-beetle stamp, do as we did – draw your own version of a scarab and have your local stamp supplier lazer cut a unique stamp for you.

136

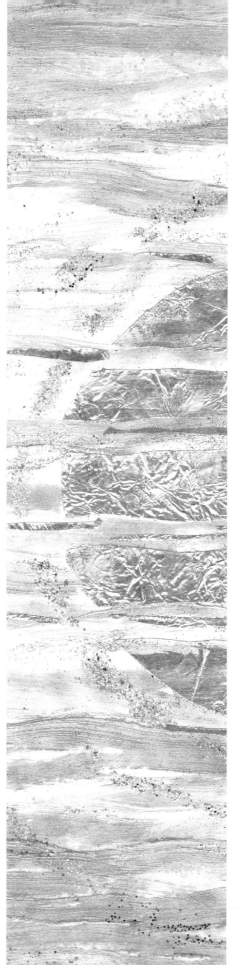

Foiled motifs

The most common method to apply foil is to use a special glue pen. We dragged gold craft paint over soft yellow card stock and drew the design in pencil. While the foil will be tacky for a while, this will wear off in time.

1 Trace the lines or fill in the areas to be foiled with the glue pen. The glue is light blue when wet; allow to dry until clear and tacky.

2 Place the foil over the tacky glue. It will come away from the backing and adhere to the glued areas. Re-glue areas where the foil does not stick, and repeat the process.

Foil can also be applied by heat. Lay a photocopy or print on a hot tray, place the foil over the copy and rub quickly with your finger. The foil will stick to the ink on the copy. If you rub too hard the foil may adhere to sections where it is not required. Use small, simple images not wider than the foil roll.

Aluminium & pearl effects

We used aluminium foil as an affordable and readily available (though not so bright) alternative to silver leaf. Find it in your kitchen drawer and glue it down or use the sticky-backed variety we found on a roll in our local hardware store – developed no doubt for some or other boring but necessary sealing job! Pearl paints are mica based and come in a wide range of colours. We used the plain pearl to soften the greyness of silver craft paint. Glitter and sparkle dust add further twinkles to this moonlit page, which would make a special greeting card for a silver anniversary.

1 Cut a circle of sticky-backed foil in strips and peel off the backing to one side as you stick them in a circle on the page, with irregular gaps between the strips. Allow the pieces to wrinkle slightly as you stick them down and then burnish them with your finger for a crinkly effect. This will catch the light better than a smooth, flat surface.

2 Paint alternate rough lines of silver and pearl craft paint between the foil strips and over the rest of the page. Use more pearl in the area around the moon, and more silver in the corners of the page to create natural wispy clouds over the moon.

3 Allow paint to dry and stick thin slivers of foil (cut from the strips not used for the circle) randomly in horizontal lines between the circle strips and above and below the circle.

4 Randomly draw horizontal broken lines with a glue stick and dust with silver sparkle dust. Allow to dry.

5 Paint some rings around the moon with wood glue, shake silver glitter over the glue and allow to dry.

6 Shake off excess dust and glitter onto a clean sheet of paper for re-use.

Computer effects

Love them or hate them, computers touch so many aspects of our lives that we can almost not get by without the many possibilities that they offer. This book would not have been written without the advantage of email, since we live in different towns. Book design is completely computer driven and in most instances dominated by digital photography. So how could we not use this wonderful tool for paper decorating too?

We used special effects, from various programs such as Microsoft Paint which is part of the Windows package on just about every computer, to the more sophisticated versions of Corel Paint Shop Pro. This book isn't about computers and their programs so we've not gone into huge detail as to how to do our examples. If this interests you, we encourage you to experiment (yet again!) with what your computer already has installed. Read the Help section installed with most programs or follow the step-by-step tutorial sequences offered by some of the more sophisticated graphics programs. We are always teaching ourselves this way.

Top right: A quick idea for using a special piece of marbled paper: cover a frame cut from mount board and slip in a moody picture to contemplate. Photo frames make easy home-made gifts for any age or occasion, so use up those odd bits of decorated paper you've been hoarding.

Right: A special gift for a teenager in love. The lid of the heart box was decoupaged with torn computer lettering (printed in negative and positive) in all the fonts and languages of love; the sides dragged with red craft paint mixed with fabric paint extender as a glaze. A worthy storage box for all those love tokens and letters read and re-read!

Bottom right: Black and white photos inkjet-printed on ordinary copy paper and pasted onto black and white card make a very special and personal set of note cards. Presented in a box covered with red painted and varnished paper, these make a stunning gift.

Opposite page: Black oil marbling on white paper was used to create a serene look for office accessories, complete with a roll of writing paper, covered pencil and notepad waiting in anticipation on a new blotter. The hexagonal pencil holder was also covered with oil marbled paper while the box file was printed with seabird feathers and white printing ink.

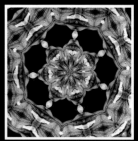

Font-filled pages

Fonts are the lettering options available in any simple Word program. If you want to manipulate your fonts as we did here, you need to work in a desktop publishing program. They offer interesting formatting options such as rotation and flip functions and are relatively easy to use. This page was created in Publisher. A themed word-page is great for cardmaking, or for scrapbookers who may use the whole page or just one word from it. The top of the heart box on page 138 was decoupaged with a sheet of love words in many languages.

1 I inserted a scanned sheet of my favourite music as the background, enlarged to fit the page by clicking the mouse onto it and dragging it to the size I needed.

2 I then made many small font boxes on the side of the page and typed one musical word into each box, using different font and size options. I even used fonts with musical names such Staccato, Allegro and Vivaldi and added a guitar for Monique and a violin for Angie!

3 When I was happy with the shapes and sizes, I dragged each word block into what I thought was the best position. I inverted and turned some of the blocks to fit them in, by clicking on the relevant rotation icon on the toolbar. This was just like doing a jigsaw puzzle!

Simple graphics

Microsoft Paint is a simple graphics program which is available to most PC users as it is part of the Windows package. We included a very basic graphic done by my digital designer daughter to show what effects you can achieve without being able to draw at all. Elizabeth Louise produces such a range in Paint we were spoilt for choice – but this one couldn't be simpler and so appealed to us! We like the idea that even three- or ninety-three-year-old hands can manage this one.

1 Open a file in Paint and click on the pencil tool. You can also choose the paintbrush tool which will offer you varying line thicknesses. Choose a colour for your line from the palette at the bottom of your screen. We selected a thin black line to scribble on a white background.

2 Wiggle the mouse and scribble all over the screen until you are satisfied with the result. Click on *Image* and choose the *Invert colours* function. A negative image of your scribble will appear – white scribbles on a black background.

This design makes an unusual background for note paper and can be printed as a negative or positive image.

Kaleidoscope paper

A gift of a more sophisticated graphics program has enabled me to play very nicely with just about every photograph I take. This was a special one, however, and not taken by me for a change but Monique's sister-in-law, Wendy Wilde. We both approve of this one of us together at our first book launch – and that is quite amazing! I decided to fiddle with the kaleidoscope feature in Corel Paint Shop Pro – a real fool rushing in where any cyberphile would hesitate to tread! And look what happened...

I cropped the bit of us which shows our favourite necklaces and then just kept playing with all the possibilities in the Kaleidoscope options. Every little change of angle and degree of rotation produced more and more exciting results. It all just about blew my mind. Real psychedelia to gladden the heart of any Sixties flower child. A variation in the kaleidoscope effects is a wrap and repeat option – by clicking on that, the most interesting patterns resulted, which reminded us of the glorious range of scrapbooking patterned paper available. So why not play and print your own if you have access to this type of program.

You do see the resemblence, don't you?

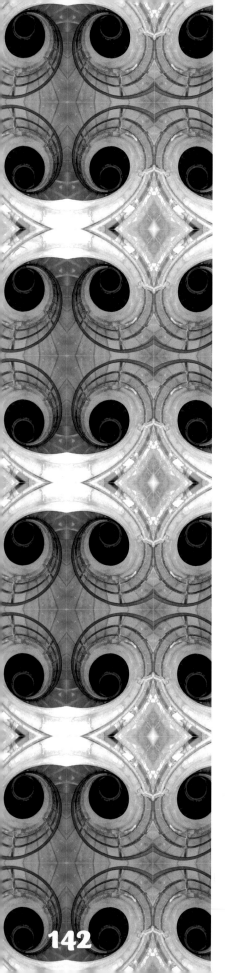

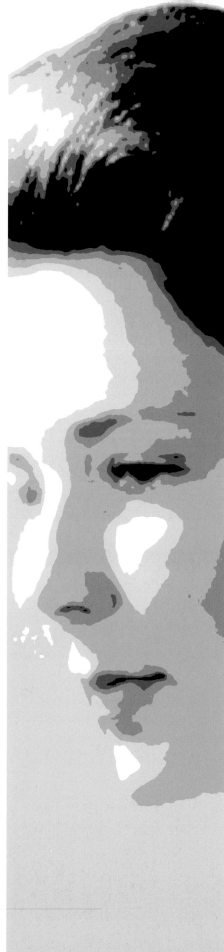

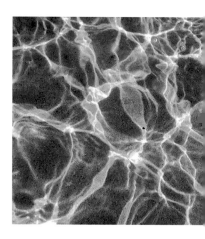

Photo patterns

Microsoft Paint is an easy option for creating photo patterns. Simple photos with little detail work best.

1 Open a file in Paint. Insert a photo by clicking on *File* and *Open*. The photo may come up large and unworkable. Change this by clicking on *Image/Stretch/Skew*. Fill in the percentage you want in the horizontal and vertical boxes and press *OK*. The image should take up no more than about an eighth of the screen.

2 Click on *Edit/Copy*, then on *Edit/Paste*. You now have two identical images. Flip the second image horizontally by clicking on *Image/Rotate/Horizontal*. Drag the rotated mirror image next to the original image. Repeat this process, now rotating the image vertically, and again, rotating it 180 degrees. Join the four images in a single picture by clicking and dragging the mouse over all four.

3 Click on *Image/Copy,* then *Image/Paste* and the picture will have been copied and pasted. Move this next to the previous one, building up a pattern. Continue across and then down the page until it has been covered and save your new creation under a new name.

Posterizing

There really is such a word (although it should be Poster Zing or Pasteurizing according to our spell check)! Posterizing is a feature on many graphics programs and one which I love to play with. It reduces a photo or image to flat planes of colour or tones as it traces the contours of patches of light and dark. This is a sophisticated form of colour separation. You can set the level of Posterizing which will determine how many tones or colours are used. In our previous book "Quick Art", we used this technique to create a "colour by number" project. The image I have used here is a picture of my aunt, Monica Hunter, who was a great influence in my life and an inspiration for this book. I used Adobe Photoshop Elements to adjust the photo.

1 Open the image in Photoshop Elements. Click on the *Filter* menu, then go to *Adjustments/Posterize.*

2 A block will come up. Fill in the level of Posterizing you require – for a picture such as the sample, we used level 7. This means that the image has been reduced to 7 different shades. You can adjust this level by changing the figure in the block. When you are satisfied, click *OK* and save your image.

Use prints of the Posterized image for personalized greeting cards or in scrapbooking.

Black-&-white photo collage

I have the most elementary digital camera which has given me much joy and generated much experimenting! These classic photographs of water, textured sand patterns, my morning beach-walk companions and our beach all make such great subjects for artistic inspiration that I have become known as our local 'mama'razzi! Crop and convert digital colour photographs into black and white beauties and mount them as sets of unique cards. Most digital cameras come with a scanning or basic photo program – read the Help instructions specific to the program to help you do this. Or download a free photo editing program (such as Picasa) off the Internet. It's simple to use and has one-step functions for many editing processes.

1 Change your pictures from colour to black and white in the *Effects* function. Use the cropping tool in *Basic Fixes* to select the best section from each photo. I selected 12 photos by clicking on the *Hold* function, and clicked *Print*.

2 Picasa let me arrange all 12 on one A4 page as wallet sized prints when I clicked on the 5 x 8 cm selection in the *Print Layout*. All I had to do then was click *Print*. You can print onto copy paper or inkjet glossy or photo paper for different effects. If you really get stuck, take your digital images to any digital printing outlet and they will do it for you – for a very reasonable fee.

Authors' acknowledgements

This book has been a truly collaborative affair and thanks must go to everyone who has had even a very small part to play. You are too many to mention by name – just know that we were blessed by your contribution. Special thanks, though, to:

Our parents, once again, for their encouragement and love.

Mike, you have indulged me in so many ways yet again!

Michael Tristan and Joshua, thanks for your patience.

Michael, again, for your continued support of our family.

John and Maria, Elizabeth Louise and Gemma, for your interest and helpful support at home.

Peter, as ever, practical, supportive and caring – words on paper aren't enough!

Carroll Reekie, Helga Langen, Jan Ganney, Lindsay Woods, Sarie Marais, Sandy Fraser, Xoliswa Yozo and the Burton, Connolly, Cook, Ehlers, Eyman, Gouveris, Klitsie, Knight, Schmidt, Tapson, Van Aarde, Wallace and Wolf families, bless you all.

Sheilagh Johnston, your help and contributions are always appreciated especially with the mosaic box.

Moira-Lee Purdon, you have been as supportive as ever.

Cherylee Jordaan, thank you for the help with the scrapbooking pages and hats - your support in so many other ways is much appreciated too.

Bernie Millar, Yolanda Watson and Carla Jordaan and friends, Heather Laithwaite – thanks for all the bead work.

Christine Moore, your mosaic picture is beautiful.

Christine Weerts and the Grade 8's at Fairmont High, thanks for the bead making. We hope the paper aeroplanes weren't too disruptive!

Tracy Boomer and Debbie Morbin, thanks for your enthusiasm and help with a couple of our scrapbooking projects.

All the ladies in our classes, thank you for your patience.

Ronelle Tyler from *Dash décor and gifts*, thank you for your space and kind hospitality.

Wilsia Metz for your professionalism as publisher and the trusted friend you've become. We really appreciate your faith in and promotion of us. Thank you to you and Ralf for opening your home to us for some interesting photographic shots – especially your Bonsais, Ralf!

Lindie Metz, for taking us on yet again and producing another wonderfully creative and cool book design! Your loft apartment was a gift as ever, for beautiful pictures.

Ivan Naudé, for the awesome photos – and the driest wit!

And last but not least, my co-author – for the gifts of untiring patience, a great sense of humour and ever-deepening appreciation, love and trust!